A GUIDE TO

CATHOLIC COLLEGE ADMINISTRATION

A Guide to

CATHOLIC COLLEGE

ADMINISTRATION

EDWARD V. STANFORD, O.S.A.
Saint Mary's Hall
Villanova, Pennsylvania

N|P

THE NEWMAN PRESS, WESTMINSTER, MARYLAND • 1965

FOREWORD

THE AUTHOR of this book has been one of the three members of the Administrative Consultant Service of the Association of American Colleges since January 1960. For almost three years he has been the doyen of the service. Over a period of five and a half years he has visited 111 colleges. As a result of his experience in dealing with the problems put to him by the presidents of these institutions he became aware that there was need for a publication which would provide guidance to many administrators in Catholic higher education. He began by writing a series of articles for one of the Catholic journals, but it soon became apparent to all of us that what was really needed was a book.

Thanks to the generosity of Lilly Endowment, Inc., whose grant has supported the Administrative Consultant since 1958, the publication of this book was made possible.

While the book is intended primarily as a help to the administrators of Catholic colleges, it will be useful to other institutions of higher education as well, both for the general administrative principles it enunciates and more particularly for the insight it offers into Catholic higher education.

We are all indebted to Father Stanford for his most effective service to the institutions he has visited, and particularly at this time for the production of this book, which is a true labor of love, over and above the call of duty.

THEODORE A. DISTLER
President Emeritus
Association of American Colleges

INTRODUCTION

For the Non-Catholic Reader

CERTAIN PRINCIPLES and problems are common to college administration in the United States no matter under what auspices a college may operate. But the application of these common principles and the solution of these common problems may well differ from college to college. This is particularly true of Catholic colleges.

In this book the writer is concerned with problems of administration as he has found them in Catholic colleges of liberal arts and sciences. Since the range of possible topics is wide, an arbitrary selection was necessary. Curricular problems have been deliberately avoided because it was thought they would take us too far afield. In choosing and developing topics we have attempted to deal with practical, rather than theoretical or philosophical matters.

It is hoped that this book will serve a double purpose—that it will be of assistance to administrators of Catholic colleges, to whom it is directly addressed, and that it will also help non-Catholic educators to understand problems that are peculiar to Catholic colleges because of the nature of their sponsorship. This twofold purpose gave rise to a minor problem.

The words religious, religious community, community, brother and sister appear frequently in this book with reference to the religious orders or congregations of the Catholic Church. These words also have a more common and general meaning. The use of the words in their specialized meaning is usually clear to a Catholic from the context, but it may be confusing to a non-Catholic. For this reason capitalization of the first letter of these

vii

words has been used in this book when they refer to the religious orders. It is hoped that this will not be an annoyance to Catholic readers, who are not accustomed to seeing these words capitalized. A reminder of the reason for this capitalization has been appended to one chapter as a footnote, where the words first appear, but has been omitted from other chapters so as not to offend by constant repetition.

The very helpful practice, now adopted by most of the regional accrediting associations, of sending large teams of evaluators to colleges which seek accreditation, is bringing an ever-increasing number of educators from non-Catholic colleges into intimate contact with Catholic colleges, many of them for the first time. Sometimes it is difficult for these men and women to understand the source of ultimate control in Catholic colleges, their administrative and financial organization, and the relative situations of lay and Religious faculty members and administrators.

Exclusive of seminaries for the priesthood and colleges open only to members of Religious Orders, there are approximately 250 four-year Catholic colleges and universities which admit lay students. Of this number only one is nationally sponsored by the Church at large. Although there are 148 administrative units, or "dioceses," of the Catholic Church in the United States, only thirteen of them operate colleges. No Catholic college is operated exclusively under lay control, although two of the diocesan colleges are staffed and administered chiefly by laymen, with the moral and financial backing of the diocese. The problem of financing and staffing these colleges is too much for laymen alone, no matter how competent and dedicated. It is too much also for the average diocese, burdened as it is with the heavy expense of meeting the ever-increasing demands for grade and high schools.

Thus it comes about that the task of operating 236 of the 250 Catholic colleges for lay students has been left to the initiative and support of the various Religious Orders or Communities, with little or no financial support from the Church itself. These Orders are more or less autonomous organizations of men and women who voluntarily bind themselves together by vows of religion. Their members are not ordinarily subject to the bishop of the diocese in which they may happen to dwell, but are governed by their own superiors under constitutions which they themselves have drawn up with papal approval. The Orders are democratically organized under a communal form of life, holding all their goods and property in common. Although living *in a diocese* of a hierarchically organized Church, they are not *of the diocese.* Their superiors are elected for fixed terms and ordinarily may be elected to succeed themselves only once. The term of office is usually three years, except for the head of the entire Order who serves a six-year term with the possibility of being reelected once. If the Order is large enough, and particularly if it is widely spread either nationally or internationally, it is organized in separate provinces, with the members of each province serving under their own elected provincial superior. Not counting provinces, there are several hundred of these separate Communities of priests, Brothers or Sisters in the United States, but no more than 130 of them are presently engaged in conducting the 236 four-year colleges mentioned above.

This is the general picture of Religious Communities and their role in the conduct of colleges. There are, of course, variations and exceptions to this pattern which are not important for our present purpose—to give a background for understanding the situation of Catholic colleges. There is far more autonomy in these Religious Communities and in their colleges than is usually realized. But there are certain built-in disadvantages that encourage a needless multiplication of colleges and make more difficult the type of collaboration between existing colleges which is so necessary today. The colleges of the different Religious Communities are only loosely drawn together on a voluntary basis through their membership in the College and University Department of the National Catholic Educational Association, which has no power to control or regulate its members except through such conditions of membership as the members themselves may voluntarily adopt.

It is the hope of the author that the considerations here presented will contribute to an understanding of the problems which are discussed in this book.

Edward V. Stanford, O.S.A.
St Mary's Hall, Villanova, Penna.

ACKNOWLEDGMENTS

THE AUTHOR has benefited from the encouragement and help of so many friends and colleagues in the production of this book that a complete listing of names will hardly be possible. He is indebted in a very special way to former President Theodore A. Distler and Vice President F. L. Wormald of the Association of American Colleges. It was Dr. Distler who requested that the book be written and gave it his earnest support and encouragement. Mr. Wormald, a non-Catholic with good knowledge and understanding of Catholic colleges, was a particularly helpful mentor. He read first and final drafts of the manuscript with painstaking care, and through his many valuable suggestions and editorial expertise made a major contribution to the book. Through its financial support of the Administrative Consultant Service of the Association, Lilly Endowment, Incorporated, provided the author with a background of experience for the book and then assisted financially in its publication.

Among the many educational colleagues who read all or most of the manuscript must be mentioned in the first place Dr. Goodrich C. White, Chancellor of Emory University. Dr. White read both the first and second drafts of the entire manuscript and was most helpful with suggestions. Other colleagues who read most of the manuscript and made helpful suggestions were: Sister M. Brendan, R.S.H.M., President of Marymount College (Tarrytown, N.Y.); Father Vincent A. McQuade, O.S.A., President of Merrimack College; Bishop James P. Shannon, President of the College of St. Thomas; and Father Robert M. Sullivan, O.S.A., Dean of Biscayne College.

Helpful suggestions were also received from the following, who read substantial portions of the manuscript: Sister M. Carolyn, R.S.M., President of Mercyhurst College; Brother Raymond Fleck,

C.S.C., President of St. Edward's University; Father Arno Gustin, O.S.B., former President of St. John's University (Minnesota); Father Stephen Herrmann, O.S.B., President of Saint Leo College; and Father Richard R. Sullivan, C.S.C., President of Stonehill College.

Chapters of the book which deal with financial and accounting matters profited from the suggestions of George E. Van Dyke, editor of the latest revision of Volumes I and II of *College and University Business Administration* and Howard Withey, head of Institutions Department of Peat, Marwick, Mitchell & Co., Certified Public Accountants. Other chapters, which touch on legal matters, were improved by suggestions received from Messrs. William B. Ball, formerly of the Law Faculty of Villanova University, and William Hall Painter and John C. Stephenson III, presently members of that faculty.

Although all of those named have made helpful contributions to this book, which are hereby gratefully acknowledged, it is the author alone who must be held responsible for all opinions and statements of fact.

Finally, the courtesy of *The Catholic Education Press* and *Prentice-Hall Incorporated,* in permitting the author to use previously published writings of his in the preparation of this book, is acknowledged with sincere appreciation.

TABLE OF CONTENTS

xiii

A GUIDE TO

CATHOLIC COLLEGE ADMINISTRATION

CHAPTER 1

The College Charter[1]

THE COLLEGE CHARTER, articles of incorporation, certificate of incorporation or whatever similar name may be used, is the legal document attesting that the state has recognized three or more persons as a "body corporate and politic" for the purpose of conducting an institution of higher learning and granting appropriate degrees and diplomas. Usually it is declared that the corporation is not organized for profit, and that it is not empowered to issue stock. The original incorporators ordinarily serve as the first governing board, to continue in office until their successors are appointed or elected, or until they become incapacitated, resign or die. The subsequent makeup of the governing board is frequently left to the bylaws which the governing board is empowered to adopt, alter, amend or annul.

Probably the foregoing paragraph comes close to being the least common denominator for the charters of the many institutions of higher education in the United States which currently enjoy the privilege of incorporation. The differences in detail of these charters are legion, however, and they vary from institution to institution and from state to state.

---

[1] This term is used throughout as synonymous with articles of incorporation, articles of agreement, articles of association, and the like.

Religious Approval

A Catholic college has both a religious and a civil character, and both Church and State have an interest in the college. The college gets its religious character when the superiors of a Religious Community[2] accede to the request of a certain bishop, or seek his approval, to found and operate a college within his ecclesiastical jurisdiction. Once agreement has been reached with the bishop, the new institution will be recognized as a Catholic college and will expect, at least, the moral support of Catholic clergy and people. Episcopal approval does not mean that the bishop assumes any direct responsibility for the college, or that the college will receive any financial support from the Church in the way that many Protestant colleges do. It is expected that the college shall be financially self-supporting. In practice this usually means that the Religious Community which operates the college must heavily subsidize it, not only through contributed services but with hard cash.

Civil Approval

The college must also qualify for state approval. That approval will come to the college only after representatives of the Religious Community, or diocesan officials in the case of a diocesan college, have complied with the requirements of the state. Through civil incorporation the state recognizes the college as a legal person entitled to certain rights and privileges, including a tax-exempt status.

Procedure for Incorporating

The actual procedure for attaining incorporation differs greatly from state to state. Various types of procedure will be mentioned here without any claim to complete coverage. In many states

---

[2] In this and succeeding chapters the words "religious community," "religious," "community," "brother" and "sister" are frequently used with particular reference to the specialized religious orders or congregations within the Catholic Church. Since these words also have a more common and general meaning, capitalization of the first letter of the words is used when they refer to the religious orders, to distinguish them from other uses of these words.

charters used to be granted to individual colleges by a special act of the legislature but this practice has almost disappeared. Instead, it is more usual for an administrative body or official to grant charters under the provisions of a general statute.

A very common procedure today is for a college to file articles of incorporation with the Secretary of State of the state wherein the college is located. In some instances the document must also be filed in the county in which the college is situated, either with the County Clerk or the Recorder of Deeds. In a few instances this latter procedure is all that is required. In Pennsylvania a preliminary certificate of incorporation is granted through a Court of Common Pleas and, upon approval of the State Board of Education, a final decree is granted. In New York a charter is granted by the Board of Regents for and on behalf of the Education Department of the State of New York, first on a preliminary basis and after a period of five years on a permanent basis. In Maryland articles of incorporation are approved and received by the State Tax Commission. In Massachusetts a college charter is granted by the state secretary but only after the articles of incorporation have been approved by the State Board of Collegiate Authority. Within the twelve years next following its approval of the certificate, "the board of collegiate authority, through its agents, shall make periodic inspection of every such educational institution." In New Mexico the State Corporation Commission has jurisdiction in the granting of college charters. In most instances college incorporation is granted in perpetuity. But a few states grant incorporation for a specific period of years with the privilege of renewing the incorporation for a further term of years at the end of that period.

Know Your Charter

A college charter is a very important document with which the president and the governing board ought to be thoroughly familiar. Sometimes a charter can lapse through the expiration of a time limit or it can be forfeited by failure to make a required periodic report. At times there may be unreasonable, even harmful, restrictions in a charter which can be removed readily by amendment. There are instances of charters that have become outmoded because needlessly detailed prescriptions were unwisely included in the original draft and have never been removed.

AN ARCHAIC PRACTICE

Some Catholic colleges do not have a charter of their own because they have never been incorporated as a separate legal entity. Frequently a Religious Community, already incorporated by the state for religious, charitable and educational purposes, found that the establishment of a degree-granting college was either necessary or highly desirable in the development of its educational work. If this contingency had not been foreseen and provided for in their original charter, frequently a new charter was not sought for the college, but instead only an enabling amendment was added to the existing charter of the Religious Community.

This was quite understandable, even defensible, a generation or more ago. But today it is archaic and out of step with the opportunities for the growth and development of these colleges. Today every Catholic college ought to have its own charter. No matter how important it may once have been for these colleges to be sheltered under a "motherhouse" charter, this is no longer necessary or desirable. The fledgling has come of age. It should have its own charter and assume its own responsibilities. Colleges have become quite complex and expensive and must be able to appeal for support more widely than in the past. When it is a separate and distinct corporation a college can make a greater appeal for support to individuals, to groups, to public and private agencies.

SEPARATE INCORPORATION IMPORTANT

The problems posed for Catholic colleges by the doctrine of separation of Church and State are more likely to prove capable of satisfactory solution, if the clearest possible distinction is drawn between the educational functions of the college and the religious functions of the Religious Community or diocese.[3]

---

[3] Thirteen Catholic colleges in the United States are operated under the auspices of dioceses rather than by Religious Communities.

Thus a separate charter is important if a college intends to contract with a government agency to do research or to render other services contracted for by these agencies. It is important also if a college wishes to take advantage of federal and state legislation which provide construction loans and grants for colleges. It is quite understandable that a federal or state agency empowered by law to contract for services by, or to make loans or grants to, higher educational institutions, would hesitate to extend such aid to a college that has no separate legal identity, but is merely one activity of an incorporated Religious Community which carries on various other activities. A separate charter for the college, with its own board of trustees, will provide a much stronger defense against the challenge to any kind of governmental assistance to privately supported colleges and universities, particularly church-related institutions. The absence of separate incorporation is a source of puzzlement and confusion not only to government agencies but also to accrediting groups as well.

The absence of a separate charter could be a handicap to the development of a college. Unless a college is separately incorporated and holds title to the land and buildings it uses, it will be handicapped in its credit by the debts and financial obligations of other schools or hospitals which may be operated under the charter of the motherhouse corporation. More than likely the legal name of a motherhouse corporation will be quite different from that of the college. This difference in name would be a handicap in the solicitation of bequests. It would be a serious drawback to any appeal for support which the college might make to prospective corporate and private benefactors. It would tend to discourage individuals, groups, and private agencies whose sole reason for interest resides in the college.

Again, there is danger for the Religious Community which heaps up the capital assets of all its activities in one civil corporation. The risk is similar to that associated with depositing all one's money in one bank. In the event of the debt or failure of one activity all could be legally involved. If, for example, there is a legal suit for damages against any institution conducted by the Religious Community, the college of that same Community could be involved. This is no minor consideration at a time when law courts are no longer recognizing exemption of charitable corporations from suits and when heavy damage judgments are being assessed against large corporations.

In brief it may be said that separate incorporation will benefit the Religious Community and will help to clarify the image and identity of the college with accrediting groups, government agencies, citizens of adjacent communities, business and industrial leaders, as well as with students, parents of students, alumni and friends—with all, in fact, who in the broadest sense can be considered among the many publics of the college. This is important, of course, if a college is to obtain the voluntary support which it needs from these various sources and continue to hold that support year after year.

LACK OF UNDERSTANDING

Many Catholic colleges have recognized the force of these reasons and have made the change in recent years. Other Religious Communities have been slow to make the change because of a hesitation to break with tradition. In some instances there really seems to be a fear that a separate corporation with its own board of trustees, holding legal title to the property used by the college, will somehow militate against the unity of the Religious Community or in some way take the college out of its control. Occasionally this fear shows up in articles of incorporation, where an attempt has been made to weld to this document provisions from the constitutions of the Religious Community.

It is important, therefore, that Religious Communities and other clerical institutions make a real distinction between the required unity of their religious organization and the necessary separation of the civil corporations which give legal existence to such important entities as colleges. A Religious Community can have under its auspices two or more civil corporations without any danger to its essential unity. The religious unity is maintained through the major religious superior and council under the Rule and Constitutions of the Community and the provisions of Canon Law. All of these are religious documents, not civil documents. On the other hand, the articles of incorporation and the bylaws of a college are civil documents which are recognized and governed by civil law and are intended for the governance of a civil institution. Furthermore, there is no reason to attempt to merge these religious and civil documents. This would result in a patchwork affair which would be quite complicated and involved and of no practical use. Members of Religious Communities are accustomed to acting in the twofold capacity of Religious and citizen. There is no problem in reconciling the two in actual practice.

AMENDING A CHARTER

The preparation of a new charter or articles of incorporation is the responsibility of the incorporators. The amending of an old one is the responsibility of the governing board. In either case the assistance of competent legal counsel is needed to insure that all be in accord with the provisions of the law as it applies to nonprofit educational corporations in each particular state. Preference should be given to a lawyer who is sensitive to the requirements of a college or who is accustomed to handling the affairs of nonprofit corporations. Although the laws of various states differ, sometimes considerably, there are certain general principles which it would be well to incorporate in each charter in so far as this is compatible with the requirements of the law.

Thus it is important to be explicit and inclusive in mentioning the legal rights and privileges of the college corporation. But it is best to deal with the governing board and the management of the college only in general terms. This allows for the preparation of bylaws which can be more specific. For example, rather than prescribe a fixed number of members for the governing board, it would be preferable to specify a minimum and maximum, and leave it to bylaws to set the number at any given time, thus permitting greater flexibility. In similar fashion bylaws could specify the manner of choosing members of the governing board, their terms, the frequency of meetings and so on.

Again, why limit by charter the activities of a college where this is not required? For example, it should be sufficient to commit a college to the work of education rather than to the education of women only or of men only. Even though the intention of a college is to serve women only, there is no need to prescribe this by charter. There are very few colleges for women today which do not enroll some men, at least in part-time or evening courses. A similar situation has long been true of men's colleges.

Occasionally, one can find college charters of fairly recent origin which read like a college catalogue. The number of professors is specified, or academic departments are named, or other academic decisions are prescribed which seem ridiculous in the light of present practice. In most of the old college charters it is interesting to note the financial restrictions by which colleges were limited in receiving, by gift, grant or otherwise, money or its equivalent in property beyond a certain fixed yearly sum. In one instance this sum was fixed at five thousand dollars a year. In many instances it was as much as twenty-five or thirty thousand dollars. These amounts were increased from time to time by amendments and finally abrogated by general statute.[4]

The point to be emphasized is this: It is wise to leave out, as far as the law will permit, such details as are likely to undergo change and require subsequent amendments. Usually the governing board is authorized by the charter "to make, ordain, establish, amend, annul or change such bylaws, rules and ordinances, not inconsistent with the Constitution and laws of the United States or of this State, as they shall deem necessary for the welfare of said institution." Or again, "in addition to the powers given them and the duties imposed upon them by law, the Board of Trustees shall also have such powers and duties as may be specified in the bylaws of the said corporation provided these are not opposed to the charter, to the Constitution and laws of the United States and of the State of _____."

WHY DISTINGUISH CORPORATION AND GOVERNING BOARD?

At times a college charter seems to make a distinction between the corporation as such and the governing board. In some instances this is carried to the extent of having two sets of officers

---

[4] There are specific procedures under which the attorney general can move to recapture for the state an endowment which may be in excess of the reasonable needs of an institution. But the problem of excessive endowments seems today fairly remote.

but the same personnel. Thus the chairman and the other officers of the corporation are also the chairman and corresponding officers of the board of trustees. Necessary or useful as this distinction may be in a commercial corporation, where there may be many stockholders, it is unnecessary and an occasion for confusion in a non-profit college corporation. Unless the law in a particular state provides otherwise, it is suggested that a college charter make it clear that "the members of the governing board of the college corporation shall constitute the members of the corporation and shall exercise, conduct and control the powers, business and properties of said corporation." In other words, it is desirable to make it clear that the members of the governing board constitute the corporation and, conversely, the members of the corporation constitute the governing board. Where confusion has arisen as to corporation and governing board, this may have been the fruit of a misguided attempt to weld constitutional provisions of the religious order to the state requirement of a civil charter.

SAMPLE CHARTERS

In the hope of crystallizing the ideas expressed in this Chapter, but with no thought of suggesting set patterns for college charters, four sample charters are given in APPENDIX I. These are the actual charters for four Catholic colleges in as many states. They have the advantage of brevity and flexibility. But they would not fulfill the requirements of the law in all states.

CHAPTER 2

The Board of Trustees

EVERY NON-PROFIT organization recognized by the state must have not only a charter of some sort but also a governing board, which may be called the board of trustees, the board of directors, the board of overseers or the like. In a few instances the governing board is known simply as "The Corporation." The charter sets forth in general terms the purpose of the organization and the rights and privileges which are guaranteed by the state. In the eyes of the state the "board of trustees" [1] holds title to the property of the organization, is ultimately responsible for its general policies, and through its approval gives a legal validity to all important transactions of that organization.

A RELIGIOUS GOVERNING BOARD

A Religious Community[2] is a non-profit organization within the meaning of civil law and is eligible for incorporation as such. From the ecclesiastical point of view, a Religious Community is governed by a "religious board of control," namely, the immediate major superior and his or her council. When this Religious Community itself, as distinct from its operational entities like a college

---

[1] The term "board of trustees" will be used throughout this chapter to designate the civil board of control.

[2] Throughout this chapter "Religious Community" is used as synonymous with religious order, religious congregation, religious society, and even diocese.

12

or a hospital, seeks incorporation in a state, it is convenient and proper for the "religious board of control" to become also the "civil board of trustees." In this situation there is no essential reason why the same group of persons cannot function successfully in the separate capacities of religious board and civil board, provided their distinct identities are kept clearly in mind. For example, the board should have one minute book when functioning as a civil governing board and another minute book when acting as the religious governing body. However, because of the dual function, there is the distinct possibility that the religious governing board may tend to forget that it is also the civil board of trustees—except when it is under a legal compulsion to act in that capacity.

DUAL JURISDICTION

A Catholic college conducted by a Religious Community, besides being governed by a civil board, has certain responsibilities to a religious board which is usually the immediate major superior of the Community and his or her council. The state recognizes only the board of trustees as the legal board of control responsible for all the corporate acts of the college. Certain acts, such as the borrowing of money, the purchase of real estate, the sale of land, etc., would have no legality without the approval of the board of trustees. The Church, however, has her own procedure and does not officially accept this approval as entirely sufficient. These same acts of the college, namely, the borrowing of money, the purchase of real estate, the sale of land, and the like, have no ecclesiastical validity without the approval of the religious board of control and sometimes of a higher religious authority.

It is to be noted that neither ecclesiastical nor civil action is contingent one upon the other. Neither does one take cognizance of the other. But it is safe to say that no Catholic college will be established at any given location, nor will money be borrowed, nor will property be purchased unless both of these distinct approvals are sought and obtained. When the separate interests of Church and State in a given college are properly understood, there need be no difficulties.

This dual jurisdiction has to a degree been responsible for the same personnel doing double duty on both the religious and the civil boards of control of a college. Confronted by the apparent diarchy, many Religious Communities did what was undoubtedly the easiest thing to do in beginning a college in the early days. If the Religious Community had already been incorporated by the state for religious, charitable and educational purposes, as mentioned in the preceding chapter, a new charter for the college was not usually considered necessary. If the existing charter was not broad enough to include a college with degree-granting powers, an enabling amendment was obtained. As a consequence the new college became one more responsibility for the board of trustees of the corporation of the Religious Community. Even in instances where a separate charter for the college was obtained, the same board of control at times became the board of trustees for the college corporation even though it was hundreds of miles away.

Conditions are quite different today. Major superiors and their councils are responsible for many more Religious subjects and for a variety of important undertakings. They can no longer give a college the personal and regular attention it deserves. Meanwhile the complexity of college operation has increased immeasurably. Assets formerly computed in the thousands of dollars are now valued in millions. Today each college needs and deserves its own functional board of trustees.

A SEPARATE BOARD OF TRUSTEES

A college should be a separate corporation and should have its own board of trustees. Trustees must assume today a greater and more intimate responsibility for the financial support and development of their colleges. In order to do this, these boards must function regularly and consistently, and must be dedicated to their task. It is doubtful, for example, that this service can be rendered efficiently by the councilors of a major superior, not because there is any lack of dedication, but chiefly because these persons would likely be preoccupied with other educational and charitable activities of the Religious Community. It could also happen that there would be little actual familiarity with the prob-

lems of higher education. There has been a notable increase in
the number of Catholic colleges which have reorganized their
boards of trustees. They have gotten away from the rigid major-
superior-and-councilors pattern, and have brought laymen on to
their boards. More than one of these colleges have testified that
this has paid dividends.

ORGANIZING A BOARD OF TRUSTEES

What should be the make-up of a board of trustees for a Catholic college? There is, of course, no hard and fast answer to this
question, which would be applicable to each and every college.
Before a college can have its own board of trustees it must have
its own charter or articles of incorporation. Sometimes the charter
specifies the number of trustees and may even prescribe other
limitations. Sometimes the charter specifies only the minimum or
maximum limits on the number of trustees. More often, there are
no special prescriptions.

In colleges owned and operated by Religious Communities,
circumstances and the nature of the Community tend to dictate
a certain pattern of organization. Certainly the board of trustees
must be so constituted that there can be no question about the
control of the college being vested in the Religious Community
which assures its existence and continued operation. This means
that at least a majority of the board members must also be members of the Religious Community. In addition, both conviction
and experience impel the author to advocate lay representation
on the board of trustees. Laymen can bring to the board knowledge and experience that will be invaluable to the college. This
representation assumes greater importance today because of the
necessity of organizing long-term "development programs." Since
many actions of the board of trustees of a college must also receive the approval of the major religious superior and his or her
council, provision must be made for full liaison between the major
superior of the Religious Community and the board of trustees.
Ordinarily this would mean that the immediate major religious
superior should serve as chairman of the board of trustees.

Finally, a Catholic college will be better served by a relatively small board of trustees which can function with ease and efficiency. This should be supplemented with an associate board of laymen. The situation is quite different in non-Catholic colleges where boards varying from twenty-five to a hundred members are usual. In a Catholic college where a majority of the members of the board must be Religious, there is no advantage in a large board—quite the contrary.

The members of the board should be selected because they can make a real contribution to the work of the board. With the exception of the major superior and the local superior they should not be chosen merely because of the position which they may hold in the Religious Community as distinct from the college, nor should they be members of the faculty. The author knows of instances where the president is not himself a member of the board of trustees but other members of the Religious Community, supposedly subordinate to the president as faculty members, are members of the board. The president can be badly hampered when it is possible for academic subordinates to sit in judgment on his actions.

Furthermore, members should be selected who can attend frequent, even monthly, meetings during the regular school year. Usually this will mean that members must be selected who reside reasonably close to the college. Any arrangement whereby trustees are comparatively remote from the college both in distance and involvement, is not satisfactory at a time when trustees in other colleges are giving greater time and attention to the development and financial support of their colleges.

When all these considerations have been taken into account, it will be apparent that a small board of trustees is the most practicable arrangement for a college operated by a Religious Community. Besides, a small board seems to help regular attendance at meetings, which is highly desirable.

Let us assume that we are to have a board of trustees composed of seven members. This seems to be a satisfactory number (if permissible under the charter). Let this board consist of three ex officio members and four elected members, a total of seven members, of whom a majority should be members of the Religious Community which operates the college. The ex officio members should be the major religious superior of the province as chairman; the local religious superior, if there is one, as vice-chairman; and the president of the college, who frequently serves as secretary-treasurer. If the president and local religious superior are one and the same person, the major superior can designate a suitable Religious to serve as the third ex officio member. The elected members, two or three of whom should be laymen, should be chosen for three-year terms by the ex officio members. Some provision should be made for overlapping terms so that all members will not go off the board at the same time. The terms of the ex officio members will be regulated by their incumbency of the offices which give them title to membership on the board of trustees.

The lay members of the board should be carefully chosen for their interest and willingness to serve the college. If one can be selected who has a legal background and another who has a financial or business background, they will contribute knowledge and service in fields where Religious are seldom proficient. These laymen will increase the competence of the board in overseeing the "big business undertaking" now connected with the operation of the average college. These lay trustees should also be able to take an active part in the continuous fund-raising activities that are now one of the ordinary functions of college administration.

Where the board of trustees of a Catholic college is relatively small and meets frequently, the committee structure common to larger governing boards in other colleges and universities is not appropriate. With the possible exception of a small finance committee to recommend or approve investments for the college's investment portfolio, no other standing committee is necessary. *Ad hoc* committees can always be appointed as required.

BYLAWS OF THE BOARD OF TRUSTEES

Usually the charter of a college gives authority to a board of trustees "to make, change, amend or annul bylaws for its own governance." In some states the bylaws must be filed with the articles of incorporation as part of the procedure for incorporation. Sometimes the articles of incorporation are so detailed in describing the board of trustees that little leeway is left to bylaws. This is regrettable. But one must observe whatever provisions the charter makes for trustees. There is always, of course, the possibility of amendment.

In any event the board of trustees should have its own bylaws (preferably approved by its own attorney), even though these repeat for the most part what has already been stated in the articles of incorporation. As far as possible, however, the bylaws should be prepared simply and should not go into unnecessary details. A sample set of bylaws is to be found in APPENDIX II of this book.

THE MINUTE BOOK

The minute book of the board of trustees is an official document that has legal status. It may be necessary to produce it in court when the college is involved in litigation. The auditing firm engaged to prepare an independent audit of accounts for the college will want to see the minute book at the very outset of its work. Here presumably, the auditors will find legal authorization for all important financial transactions of the college. Accrediting groups and evaluation teams are giving increasing attention to the completeness and adequacy of the minutes of the board of trustees.

Through the minute book it should be possible to trace all important transactions of the board from their inception to their conclusion. The minutes should also reflect the concern of the board for the academic problems of the college as well as for the financial problems. The minute book is, therefore, a very important document and should be carefully kept. Since everyone does not have the knack of taking good minutes, someone other than a board member ought to be co-opted to take minutes for the official secretary of the board. Some may prefer the use of a tape recorder. It is particularly difficult for a trustee to participate in discussion and at the same time take minutes. If a typed draft of the minutes is prepared immediately after each meeting, copies can be sent to board members for their corrections, if any, by a specified date. A final draft of the minutes can then be formally approved by the board as a whole at their next meeting and be carefully recorded in the minute book.

SHARED CONTROL

There is another pattern to be found in the governing boards of a relatively few Catholic colleges, which the author mentions but does not recommend generally. It is a form of "shared" control. Under this type of governing situation the corporate body (presumably small) has full charter authority to create another body (presumably larger) to which it can delegate all, or most, or part of the legal powers as it may see fit. The following excerpt from a charter granted to a Catholic college by the general assembly of its home state will illustrate the point:

> The said corporation shall have the power and authority to create a subordinate board under any appropriate name to be composed of such number of persons, either members of the corporation, or other persons, or partly of such members and partly of such other persons as the corporation shall from time to time determine. Said corporation may confer on said board such corporate power and duty as it sees fit and it may alter, amend, change, revoke or annul said powers and duties in any manner it shall see fit.

In this instance the corporation, which consists of three persons and is known as "the corporation," is really the primary board of control. It has appointed a larger and subordinate body, known as the "board of trustees," to which it delegates most of its legal powers. Here there is a real distinction between the corporation and the board of trustees. Both corporation and board of trustees have legal authority, the parent group by inherent right, the board at the pleasure of the parent group.

It would seem that this arrangement might serve a useful function in a Catholic college under diocesan control. A college corporation with minimum membership of which the bishop would be chairman, could delegate the ordinary powers of overseeing the operation of the institution to a larger and predominantly lay board of trustees. This board could meet frequently and regularly under the guidance of definite bylaws. For practical purposes this board would function in most cases as a governing board.

Under such an arrangement it should ordinarily be possible for the corporation to transact its legal business at one yearly meeting. Since members of the board of trustees would not ordinarily be members of the corporation, at least the president of the college ought to be a member of both the corporation and the board of trustees in order to insure proper liaison.

INSURANCE FOR SURVIVAL

Whatever pattern of legal organization a college may follow, it is of the greatest importance that the governing board be set up in such a way that it will be functional, and can command the help and support of as large a group of laymen as possible. The years ahead give every promise of being difficult and stormy for privately supported colleges. Those colleges which fail to strengthen their legal organization and to enlist the interest and support of dedicated laymen will have no one to blame but themselves if they run into difficulties which they cannot surmount.

In addition to a sound legal organization, church-related colleges ought to have some way of keeping up with potentially harmful legislative trends and developments. These colleges are not only affected by some requirements of federal statutes and decisions of the federal courts but also must take cognizance of what is going on in their own states. In every one of the fifty states case law created by decisions of state and local courts, a growing body of statute law enacted by the state legislature, and administrative regulations promulgated with the force of law by regulatory agencies, can affect church-related colleges.

For some years now the American Council on Education has rendered an excellent service in keeping tabs on federal legislation and administrative regulations of federal agencies which are of concern to higher education. It regularly makes representations to the federal government when necessary, and keeps the colleges fully informed. Something similar is needed on the state level—

an office or organization, one of whose functions is to keep abreast of all litigation, bills in the legislature, and regulatory proposals on the state level, which are likely to affect the interest of church-related colleges.

CHAPTER 3

The Associate Boards

AMERICAN INSTITUTIONS of higher education have always felt the need for voluntary lay assistance. In the past non-Catholic colleges have found this assistance through their boards of trustees. These boards have on the average about twenty-five to thirty members, although some range as high as a hundred members. The membership of the usual college board of trustees presents a good cross section of successful men of affairs. Bankers and business men, judges and lawyers, industrialists and men prominent in civic life, as well as men from other walks of life, consider it an honor and privilege to be elected to the board of trustees of a college. These men, for the most part, take membership on these boards very seriously and render service of incalculable value to the colleges.

Of recent years many colleges, even those with the largest boards of trustees, have felt the need of involving a greater number of voluntary lay helpers. They have organized a variety of auxiliary or associate lay boards, some on a purely advisory basis, others to serve certain limited or specialized purposes. There seems to be no great problem in recruiting members for these boards. Although these boards or groups do not have the legal authority or responsibility of boards of trustees, they can and do render important services to the colleges.

This is a significant development which should be of interest to administrators of Catholic colleges. They, for many years, have felt the need to recruit auxiliary or associate boards of laymen to make up for the limitations of their own boards of trustees. But frequently these boards have been ineffective because they have not been properly recruited or organized.

Need for an Associate Board

The board of trustees of the average Catholic college is ill equipped for the type of fund-raising necessary for colleges today. Such a board has very few members—five or seven as a rule. At least a majority of these trustees will be Religious, who could hardly carry on a development program (including fund raising) without substantial assistance from outside. One way to meet the problem is to form an associate board of laymen, carefully screened and selected, who are definitely interested and willing to assist the college. This associate board should be able to make up for the deficiencies of a predominantly Religious board of trustees. Catholic colleges will have to depend more and more on these associate boards for substantial help in the long-term development and support of the college.

More than an Advisory Board

In many instances in the past, Catholic colleges have included in their catalogue advisory boards that were little more than lists of prominent men or women. Membership was readily accepted because no work was involved. It was nice for the member of the advisory board to be able to say that he served on the advisory board of Mythical College. For its part the college was apt to feel that listing the names of prominent persons in the catalogue was good public relations. Where there have been no definite terms for appointment to such an advisory board, it is difficult to get rid of the dead wood and to reorganize the board as a working group committed to the development of the college. This, however, has to be accomplished, because the board of trustees needs collaborators who are willing to give of their experience, time, and money, where possible, to assist with planning, fund raising and all that concerns the advancement of the college.

If, upon analyzing the current "advisory" board listed in its catalogue, a college should find that this board is not suitable as a working group, all is not lost. If it is not practicable to drop this advisory board or to remake it as a suitable working board, then, in the interest of peace and harmony, the trustees should retain it until it dies a natural death. In the meantime, they can recruit a new and carefully selected board with a different and appropriate name, which has the willingness and capacity to collaborate with the board of trustees in all that pertains to the development of the college. It may be possible to include one or two persons from the old group who meet this requirement and add them to the new board.

ESTABLISHING THE ASSOCIATE BOARD

Provisions for the associate board should be made in the bylaws of the board of trustees. There its general character and functions can be outlined, with the proviso that within this general framework the associate board many draw up its own bylaws. (See Appendix II, page 194). It should have its own chairman and secretary, although the president of the college probably should appoint a member of his own staff to serve informally as a nonvoting executive secretary to get out notices of meetings, keep the minutes, and handle other details.

All appointments to the associate board should have the approval of the board of trustees and should be for a definite term, three years or more, with the possibility of reappointment after a year's interval. The reason for the interval of a year before reappointment is to make it easier to drop inactive members without giving offense or seeming to make distinctions. The year's interval will also prevent reappointments from becoming perfunctory. Some college administrators have feared the possibility of losing a very active and dedicated member through this procedure. But those who have used this method give assurance that the college does not lose the really dedicated member, since he can serve the college in many ways during the interval and will appreciate all the more his reappointment to the board.

It is important that a prospective member of the associate board should understand that he is being invited to join a working board, and should know beforehand just what will be expected of him as a member. Moreover he should be selected not only for his interest and competence as an individual, but also for his ability to work harmoniously with the group.

It sometimes happens that a valued friend, who may be deeply committed to the college and who is able and willing to render devoted service in an individual capacity, would never be able to work as a member of a group. Such a person should never be selected as a member of the associate board. His dominating personality could kill off the initiative of the other members. To guard against this possibility, it is well to make certain beforehand that all prospective members of the board are acceptable to the current members. This is, of course, a vital consideration in forming a new board.

The members of such a board should be on a comparable social and intellectual level so that they will hold each other in mutual esteem and will be glad of the opportunity of being associated together in working for the college. This does not mean, of course, that they must all be members of the same country club, all Democrats or all Republicans, all Catholics or all Protestants. In the absence of lay members on the board of trustees, a small group of men personally known to, and mutually esteemed by, one another could be selected to form the nucleus of an associate board, and their advice should be sought in recruiting additional members.

With these considerations in mind some college presidents have made it their practice, once a prospective member has been favorably approved, to extend an invitation to membership on the board only through a personal interview with the prospect. In this way the purpose of the board can be made clear, questions can be dealt with immediately, and the prospective member can be given the opportunity to think the matter over before indicating his reaction. If he indicates that he is willing to serve, he can then be extended a formal invitation in writing.

TITLE OF THE ASSOCIATE BOARD

Associate boards currently appear under a variety of names. No particular name is proposed here. But talks with members of these boards at various colleges indicate that neither the word "lay" nor the word "advisory" should be part of the title of an associate board. Although the board is intended to be made up predominantly of laymen, the use of the word "lay" in the title seems to imply an invidious distinction between "lay" and "cleric" or "lay" and "Religious." Again, although it is technically true that the authority of an associate board is, in the final analysis, "advisory," the use of this word in the title seems to create a psychological block to the initiative and confidence of the board. The members of an associate board are fully conscious of the extent of their authority and should not be constantly reminded.

In choosing a title for this associate board, therefore, one must not emphasize that it is *merely* an advisory board. On the other hand one must not give the impression that it is the legal governing board. Within these limitations the names "Associate Board," "President's Council," or "Board of Visitors," seem to be acceptable. Where the legal governing board is known as "The Corporation," the associate board might even bear the title, "Board of Trustees."

COMPOSITION AND SIZE OF BOARD

The composition and size of the associate board will depend a great deal on local circumstances. The number of members might range between twelve and twenty or more. As far as possible, the membership of the board should be reasonably well balanced with men from various walks of life. It should be made up chiefly, if not entirely, of laymen. There is no reason why there should be any religious restrictions on membership. In many cases the membership should be predominantly, if not entirely, local. In other instances a board of the stature required would not be possible with only local membership. However, the wider the geographical distribution of membership, the more difficult it is to maintain a "working" board.

At least the president of the college and the lay members of the board of trustees should be ex officio members of the associate board. Since this board must work closely with the trustees, the president and the lay trustees can be an effective liaison. The lay trustees, especially, can help to interpret the college to the associate board, and the associate board to the college, and advise the president and other college officers in all relations with the associate board. From time to time other officers of the college, and appropriate faculty members, could be invited to attend particular meetings. Occasionally joint meetings of the board of trustees and the associate board could be held.

FUNCTIONS OF AN ASSOCIATE BOARD

An associate board should be concerned principally with ways and means of promoting the expansion and development of the college by enhancing its public relations, advising on its financial management, and assisting in raising funds for current operations, endowments, scholarships, building projects and the like. In fulfilling these functions the board should be empowered both to review proposals submitted to it by the board of trustees and to initiate proposals for the consideration of the board of trustees. It ought to be made clear that any individual member, without the necessity of a formal meeting of the board, should feel free at any time to respond to the request of the president of the college for advice on any matter pertaining to the college. In addition to its general organization the board should be organized into sub-committees so that tasks are spread evenly and everyone has some responsibility. Just what these committees should be will depend on circumstances and the composition of the board. There is no fixed pattern that is generally applicable.

Thus if there are two or three members of this board who understand investments, they could be constituted as a finance or investment committee to keep an eye on the investment portfolio of the college and advise as to purchase and sale of securities.

Even though the college employs a trust company or an investment service, it would be advisable for this investment committee of the associate board to review the investment holdings of the college periodically. This would be a beneficial check on the service being rendered by a commercial agency.

If there are members of the board who are likely to be consulted on the making of wills, such as lawyers and insurance men, they could constitute a committee on bequests to work on a bequest program for the college. They could be authorized to co-opt other suitable helpers outside the associate board to join them in this work.

Public relations men, newspaper publishers or editors could make up a committee on public relations. Architects and builders could form a small committee on buildings and grounds. Accountants and business men could serve as a committee on business management, to review the work of the business office, purchasing methods, financial reports and the like. In a word, these small committees of two or three members can be organized to suit both the composition of the board and the needs of the college.

These sub-committees ought to be encouraged to hold meetings at their own convenience, either at the college or away from the college. Let them discuss their findings and recommendations with the president and then report at a meeting of the entire associate board. Under a committee form of organization two meetings a year will usually be found adequate for the full board. If the sub-committees are expected to report at each of these meetings, this of itself will be an incentive for them to be active and will also provide the initial agenda for the bi-annual meetings. One associate board, operating on this basis, had very active sub-committees, which came to the general meetings with so many projects to involve the activities of the whole board that the chairman had to set up a committee to recommend an order of priority for these projects. Needless to say, this was a functioning associate board.

It should not be assumed, of course, that all this activity is self-propelled. There has to be an executive secretary, who may be also the director of development or assistant to the president— preferably a competent layman or a laywoman, who can win the confidence and respect of the board members and keep constantly in touch with the officers of the board and the chairmen of sub-committees. In being willing to furnish whatever information or services these members may require, this college staff officer can also serve as a gentle reminder of meetings to be held and of assignments to be fulfilled.

INVOLVING THE BOARD

No matter how well selected an associate board may be, no matter how interested, willing and able its members, this will not insure involvement in the college. The board members can fulfill their function to serve the college only insofar as this is made possible for them by the administration of the college. They must be made to feel that they are really an important part of the college. They should understand the objectives of the college and its hopes and plans for the future. They must be supplied with a continual stream of meaningful reports and memoranda. They should receive periodic reports on the finances of the college as well as the auditor's annual report. Their interest must be personally cultivated. They should receive invitations to all public functions of the college such as commencements, convocations, concerts, lectures and the like, and should have an honored place when they come. The executive secretary of the board should see that all these details are taken care of. But the president of the college himself should be in constant touch with selected members of the board by telephone and by personal visit, when there is a legal problem to discuss, an insurance problem, a real estate problem, a public relations problem and the like. The director of development (if he does not happen to be serving as executive secretary) must keep in touch with committees and committee chairmen of the board.

Bringing the members of the associate board together once or twice a year for a dinner meeting to listen to reports from various college officials, or to hear partial reports on finances, or to hear presented certain selected needs of the college or certain selected problems on which the administration has already pretty much made up its mind, or to hear for the first time about the purchase or sale of an important tract of land or the signing of an important contract as a *fait accompli*—these are the things that would frustrate any associate board worthy of the name.

Nevertheless such things have happened. An associate board whose members had been asked to consider whether or not the college ought to think of acquiring a larger campus outside the city, were astonished one day to read in the morning paper a real estate dealer's announcement that he had sold a certain tract of land to the college. In another case an associate board had been engaged in raising funds for a much needed building, only to find out by chance that the money thus far raised had been withdrawn from the bank as a temporary loan to another operation of the Religious Community, without benefit of any consultation with them. In such instances, if the board does not in fact dissolve, it is understandable why the members have no feeling of involvement.

Avoid Spreading Efforts too Widely

We have been concerned in this chapter chiefly with the type of associate board that is intended to co-operate directly with the board of trustees in the broad development program of the college, as that kind of program is currently understood. An interested and capable associate board, whatever its name, is essential and central to the success of a well-conceived development program. But such a program will never get off the ground unless it gets maximum support from the board of trustees, which has in the final analysis the legal responsibility for planning and for raising, or causing to be raised, the funds required for the operational and capital expenditures of the college. Although the associate board has no *legal* authority, its members may actually have as much—or more, influence in the operation of the college as the trustees of many non-Catholic colleges. If the members of the associate board do not have such influence, they are not fulfilling their proper function.

It may be that there are other and more specialized areas in which a college feels the need of outside professional advice and assistance. This may be the case, for example, with its research program, with the organization and curricula of its engineering program or its business administration program, and so on. In such instances there is no reason why the college should not have other appropriate boards, or councils, or committees, as circumstances may require. This would seem to be more efficient than to expect one associate board to include a span of activity that is too wide and varied.

CHAPTER 4

The Distinctive Objectives of a College

EVERY COLLEGE ought to have a clear, practical and specific statement of objectives. This statement ought to tell what the college is trying to do and should serve to motivate, not only the work of the college itself, but also the efforts of all who are connected with it. Such a clear statement of objectives has been given added urgency of late years, because the regional accrediting associations have made the objectives of a college the focal point of their evaluative procedures. Moreover, they expect the statement of objectives of a particular college to be distinctive of that college.

Some Catholic colleges have found it difficult to prepare a statement of objectives that meets the expectations of the regional accrediting associations for definiteness. Especially do these colleges find it difficult to understand why it is apparently taken for granted that the statement of objectives of one Catholic college should be clearly distinguishable from each and every other Catholic college. Let us try to analyze this difficulty and to clear up such misunderstanding as may exist. It may be helpful, first of all, to comment on the philosophy of the regional accrediting associations.

32

Philosophy of the Regional Accrediting Associations

The current philosophy of the regional accrediting associations is based essentially on the principle: "Let the college state its specific objectives and then set forth its considered and honest opinion as to how well it is meeting these objectives." This is the so-called "self-study," the college's own self-evaluation of its work. This self-study must precede the visit of a team of educators from sister colleges, whose members make an objective evaluation of the college in the light of this self-study and their own direct observations.

It is the function of this "visiting team" to form an opinion as to how well the college is meeting the objectives which it has voluntarily set for itself. In order that this opinion may be as impartial as possible, the visitors are expected to forget how things are done in their own institutions and try to make an unprejudiced judgment as to how far this particular college is attaining *its own stated objectives*.

This theory of accrediting—as far as is humanly possible—places all kinds and types of colleges on an equal footing for accrediting purposes. It should be particularly agreeable to Catholic colleges. In its conception it is sound and eminently fair. The actual working out of the theory in practice is conditioned, of course, by the human element. How definitely and accurately can a college analyze and state its objectives, and how well can it present its actual performance? On the part of the visiting committee a lot depends on how successfully the members individually can divest themselves of potential prejudices and preconceived notions as to how they think a college ought to be run. Then they must strive to give an impartial appraisal as to how this particular college is being conducted in the light of its own statement of objectives and its own policies and methods.

Clear Statement of Objectives Important

This philosophy of accrediting emphasizes how important it is for each college to state its objectives definitely and clearly. The making of such a statement seems to be a stumbling block for many Catholic colleges. Especially is a Catholic college puzzled when told that its statement of objectives is "so idealistic and general that it would apply to almost any college," and that "there is nothing in the statement of objectives which explains why this particular college was established, or why it is distinctive or different from any other Catholic college."

In order to appreciate what substance there is for this kind of criticism, all one has to do is to look through a recent file of the catalogues of Catholic colleges. The chances are that the statements of objectives will be brief and surprisingly similar in content. There will be mention of the education of the whole man; the training of the perfect Christian; fidelity to the liberal arts tradition; and the reinforcement of Catholic belief and practice. The statement will be attested by a quotation or a paraphrase from the encyclical letter of Pius XI on the *Christian Education of Youth*. Occasionally, one will find a quotation from Cardinal Newman's *The Idea of a University*.

How Can the Objectives of Catholic Colleges Differ?

Why should Catholic colleges be expected to be different from each other? As Catholic colleges, do they not have much in common? Do they not all subscribe to the same philosophy of life, the same doctrinal and moral teaching? It may be conceded that there are certain differences in traditions, spirit, and atmosphere, which are characteristic of colleges conducted by the different Religious Communities. One can distinguish, perhaps, Benedictine Colleges, Jesuit Colleges, Augustinian Colleges, Franciscan Colleges, and so on. But how can colleges conducted by the same Religious Community be distinctive and different? All Jesuit colleges, for example, have many things in common. This is true also for the colleges conducted by any other Religious Community.

When the statement of objectives of a Catholic college has been criticized for not being sufficiently distinctive, a request is sometimes made for a sample statement of objectives for a college that is considered to be satisfactory. The reply has been made that this would not help, because the objectives of no two colleges can be exactly alike. Each college must work out for itself its own individual statement of objectives. This is a task that no one but the college itself can undertake. Only the faculty, administration, and governing board of the individual college can state officially the objectives for that college. In other words, the expectation is that no two colleges, conducted under any auspices, will be exactly alike.

Defining Terms

The author believes that if one will make an attempt to define the terms that are being used by accrediting associations, much light can be thrown on the seeming dilemma. Thus the *objectives* of a college can be interpreted to mean the *commitments* of a college. It seems evident that no two colleges will have identically the same commitments. Take, for example, the eight or nine colleges conducted by the Sisters of Mercy of the Union. Certainly, these colleges of the Sisters of Mercy have a number of commitments in common. They are all Catholic colleges, all are liberal arts colleges, and all are colleges for women. But they also have individually, different commitments, which may stem from the diocese in which they are established, the town, city, or state in which they are located, the type of students that they seek to enroll, and so forth.

If the *sum total* of their individual commitments is considered, it seems clear that no two colleges of the Sisters of Mercy will be exactly alike. Each can be considered a distinctive college and different from every other college of the Sisters of Mercy, because the sum total of the commitments of each college is different from the sum total of the commitments of any of the other colleges.

Preparing a Statement of Objectives

We have already indicated that the statement of objectives for any college should be the composite result of the efforts of faculty, administration, and governing board. According to the suggestions to be found in the manuals of the regional accrediting associations, the self-study of a college should result initially from the work of several committees. One of these should be the Committee on Objectives. Presumably their function is to examine critically the existing statement of objectives, consider whether it is currently suitable for the college, make recommendations for revision or prepare a new statement of objectives, as the situation may seem to demand.

The author has had occasion to read several reports which have issued from these "Committees on Objectives." At the risk of generalizing from particular statements, he concludes that most of these committees tend to misunderstand and exaggerate their function by attempting to present their ideas of a Catholic philosophy of education and their defense of the same. As a consequence, a statement of objectives may be too lengthy and too theoretical, with little concern for the day-to-day operation of the college. True enough, a coordinating or an editing committee is supposed to cut it down to size and bring it into conformity with the over-all scope of the self-study. Frequently this is an almost impossible job without a complete rewriting of a more suitable statement.

A Practical Statement

The statement of objectives which is now considered suitable for a college ought to be a practical rather than a philosophical statement. It must comprise every commitment which the college accepts, or is in the process of accepting. It should furnish a reason for everything that a college is now doing, or trying to do. Every policy, every academic course, every curricular or extra-curricular undertaking, every service which the college renders to its enrolled students, to its alumni, to other educational institutions or to public or private groups should be able to be traced back to the official statement of objectives.

What are, for example, the objectives of the college for its own students? Why does the college make theology and philosophy core subjects in the curriculum? Why does it have a health program? Why does it encourage both intramural and intercollegiate athletics? Why does the college offer evening courses for people in the community both on a credit and non-credit basis? Why does it offer part-time courses to teachers in the community? Why does the college affiliate with itself a novitiate or a juniorate of its own Religious Community or that of another Community? Why does it give or not give certain professional courses? As a liberal arts college, why does it give certain secretarial, home economics, or business courses?

Another angle of approach would be to list what the college considers to be its various commitments. Is it committed to be a Catholic college and what flows from this? Is it committed to be a men's college, a women's college, or a coeducational college? Is it committed to be a liberal arts college? Does it feel that it has any commitment to the Catholic diocese in which it is located, to the city, town, state or community in which it is located? Does it have an obligation to the Religious Community which founded it and contributes largely to its support? Does it feel that it is obligated to any particular type or class of students: the average, the above average, the less than average student, the rich student, the poor student, the middle-class student? If so, what follows from each one of these commitments? What policies, practices, courses, activities can be traced back to each of the acknowledged commitments?

The Catholic college which wishes to test the adequacy of its present statement of objectives should try to find therein a reason for everything that it is now doing. One should be able to deduce various college policies from these objectives—for example, the place of lay faculty, the college's admission policy, its attitude towards the guidance and discipline of its students. Unless all this can be done clearly, its statement of objectives cannot be considered adequate under the current philosophy of the regional accrediting associations.

An Illustration

A statement of objectives that is peculiar and proper to the individual college can be drawn up only by those who are associated with that college. But in order to illustrate and make clearer what has been said here, it may be helpful to consider an imaginary college and to write for it a partial statement of objectives.

It is not intended to be a typical college, much less is it the ideal college. It has arbitrarily been assigned commitments which are both typical and atypical, the better to illustrate the method of stating objectives.

Let our imaginary college be known as Mythical College. It is a liberal arts college for women, established fifty years ago, conducted by a Religious Community of women, located in a small town where it is the only institution of higher education within a radius of seventy miles. The college enrolls approximately six hundred full-time students and has approximately three hundred part-time students, both men and women. There is also a summer school which enrolls almost four hundred students, most of whom are teachers. A limited amount of work is offered for the master's degree through the part-time and summer courses.

In a neighboring town about seven miles distant, the motherhouse of the Religious Community is located. Here are the novitiate and juniorate of the Religious Community. A few classes are held for novices at the motherhouse but the junior Sisters regularly attend classes at the college, being transported to and from by bus. Thirty miles away from the college is the motherhouse of another Religious Community of women, whose Sisters teach in many grade schools and two high schools of the diocese. The motherhouse of this Religious Community, which has no college of its own, is recognized as a branch or center of Mythical College. The faculty is composed of lay teachers from Mythical College and three or four qualified Sisters of this neighboring Religious Community who have been added to the faculty of Mythical College. Mythical College closely supervises and accepts full responsibility for the work at this center. With this description of Mythical College in mind, the following statement of objectives is proposed.

OBJECTIVES OF MYTHICAL COLLEGE

Mythical College has set for itself the fulfillment of objectives which arise from the following commitments, which the College clearly recognizes and fully accepts.

Thus:

Mythical College is a Catholic college, thereby committed to upholding a Catholic philosophy and way of life. For this reason philosophy and theology are considered core subjects and are prescribed in all curricula. Full opportunity for Catholic religious worship and for participation in the sacramental life of the Church are provided at the college. A resident chaplain is constantly available for consultation by students. Since qualified non-Catholics are welcomed as students, suitable adjustments are made for them in the requirements for certain theology courses and in attendance at religious worship.

Mythical College is a liberal arts college committed to upholding the liberal arts tradition in higher education. The college insists on a substantial proportion of courses in the basic academic disciplines even in curricula intended to be vocational or professional in emphasis.

Mythical College is primarily a women's college. Consequently the physical facilities have been designed with women particularly in mind. Dormitory accommodations are available only for women. The curricula for full-time students have been designed especially for women. The physical education and health program, the various extracurricular activities, and all the regulations have been planned especially for women. The college does, however, accept qualified men students in evening, part-time, and summer sessions.

Mythical College believes it has a mission to students with average and even less than average preparation for college. The area in which the college is located is largely rural, and many students come from homes in which little English is spoken. For this reason its entrance requirements are designed to be realistic and flexible rather than rigid.

Mythical College acknowledges a special commitment to the Congregation of Mythical Sisters which founded and still generously subsidizes the College. For this reason every possible collaboration and accommodation is extended to this Community in the education of the Sisters who may teach at the college or at any of the many primary and secondary schools of the diocese.

Mythical College, as part of the educational system of the Diocese of _____, recognizes a commitment to do everything possible to assist in the training of teachers, particularly for the schools of the diocese. Saturday classes, summer school, limited graduate work, and also an extension center have been undertaken in fulfillment of this commitment.

Mythical College feels a particular commitment to the town of _____ and the surrounding communities and towns, whose citizens have always shown deep interest and pride in the college and have assisted it in many ways. For this reason the college provides in-service courses for teachers in the public schools, both men and women, offers adult educational courses in the evenings, and makes available to residents of the surrounding communities various lectures and programs in the performing arts.

— — —

There is no particular virtue in the order in which these objectives have been listed. The order which seems to give the entire statement strength and coherence should be preferred. It should also be noted that the commitments are not necessarily typical. It may be that these commitments have been illustrated in greater detail than might be either necessary or desirable in the case of an actual college. This has been done to make doubly clear that the statement of objectives furnishes a basis for everything that Mythical College is doing.

It should be evident that the sum total of these objectives quite definitely distinguishes Mythical College from all other colleges, even from colleges which may be conducted by the same Religious Community in other sections of the country.

CHAPTER 5

The Role of the President

WHILE THE board of trustees is legally responsible for an American college as a corporate entity—for its property, operation, and welfare—the board customarily concentrates its attention on formulating general policies and overseeing the financing and development of the college. This is normally done with the assistance and counsel, often with the guidance or under the leadership, of the president. The board's responsibility for day-to-day operation is substantially delegated to the president who, as chief executive officer of the college, is charged with implementing its policies and acting as a two-way channel of communication between the board and the administration, faculty, and students. The selection of a president for the college is considered one of the chief tasks of the board.

THE CHIEF EXECUTIVE

The president, as the educational leader and chief executive of the college, is responsible for all its activities. While widely delegating duties and responsibilities to others, he must himself furnish educational leadership, always be in touch with what is going on, and assure himself that all policies established by the board of trustees are fully implemented. It is his responsibility to see that all legal requirements are met; that everything possible

41

is done to promote the best interests of students and faculty and to attain the stated objectives of the college. As the official head, the president is expected to represent the college to its constituencies, to the general public, to educational groups and agencies, and, in general, to be the spokesman of the college in all its external relations.

The president of a college is held in high repute by the American public. No other administrative position in a college carries as much weight and potential influence as the presidency. There is considerable prestige attached to the very name of president, which is not accorded to any other college title, like vice president or dean. The word "president" is an open sesame in many circles. A college president receives invitations to functions and meetings that are closed to others. On many occasions there are meetings for college presidents only, meetings which are quite important to a college and to which the president is invited with the explicit understanding that he may not send a substitute. An American college president needs all the prestige and influence he can muster to carry on with a fair share of success the arduous duties that fall to his lot. Yet some Catholic college presidents have been obliged to function under conditions that undermine the influence and prestige of their position and handicap the college.

There is no essential reason why the role, the prestige, or the influence of the president of a Catholic college should differ from that of colleagues in other colleges. If it does differ, this happens either because major religious superiors do not have a proper understanding of the president's situation or because the customs, traditions or practices of the Religious Community controlling the college have been slow to adjust to the growing complexity of college administration. We will discuss briefly a few handicaps which still confront the presidents of some Catholic colleges.

In Fact or in Name?

In a few instances the actual, functioning head of the college bears the title of dean, or executive vice president. Meanwhile the title of president is held by a major religious superior or a diocesan official, as a recognition of an ecclesiastical position or as an honorary mark of esteem. This is not only a great disservice to the college, but it is a handicap as well to the one who must undertake the functions of a college president. A college stands to lose something in stature, prestige, and representation when its active administrative head does not have the title to indicate his position. If one has complete responsibility for heading a college but lacks the title of president, he or she will hardly ever be accepted in educational circles on a parity with one who bears the title of president.

There seems to be no reason why the title of president should be held by anyone other than the actual head of the college. Every college has a board of trustees which bears full legal responsibility for the college, and it is appropriate that the chairman of this board should be the major religious superior. But it is quite indefensible to have a president of a college with either a major or a local superior behind the scenes, whose voice is decisive on all college affairs and who must be consulted on everything. For the welfare of the college, as well as for the peace of mind of administrative officers and faculty members, it would be far better for such a superior to hold both jobs openly and to accept full presidential responsibility. While this would not be desirable in itself (as the author points out later), it would be the lesser of two evils.

The staff of a Catholic college is no longer a self-contained Religious Community. Lay people, including teachers, secretaries, maintenance and service staffs, greatly outnumber the members of the Religious Community. A college president must deal with them all, especially with students, lay and religious teachers, educational agencies, government agencies, sister colleges, and the general public. In the eyes of all those who are not members of the Religious Community, the one who has the title of president is presumed to have the powers and responsibilities usually associated with that position. It can be very puzzling and unsettling to lay people in the employ of the college, when they come to discover that there is another person on the campus who wields greater authority than the college president. It is also very embarrassing and unfair to the one who bears the title of college president. And it is impossible to explain this situation to outsiders, to educators from other colleges, to representatives of accrediting agencies, to business men, or even to alumni and friends of the college.

Fortunately, today, the great majority of the priests, Brothers, and Sisters who head Catholic colleges have the same formal authority and acknowledged responsibility as their colleagues in other colleges. For the most part these Catholic educators are well able to administer their own colleges and can hold their own with any other presidents.

In recent years, in Catholic women's colleges especially, there has been remarkable development in the ability and accomplishments of the religious administrators. It once seemed to be the rule that Sisters were to be seen and not heard at educational meetings, whether exclusively Catholic or not. Even at their own commencement exercises they sat with the audience and let others front for them. Today the Sisters who staff colleges need no one to front for them or to prompt them from behind the scenes. They have become outstanding leaders in the development and progress of their colleges.

PART-TIME PRESIDENT

Fifteen or twenty years ago comparatively few Catholic colleges recognized the need for any distinction between the local religious superior and the administrative head of the college. Both positions were held by one and the same person. But as colleges increased in complexity and enrollment, it became an impossible burden for any one to be saddled with both responsibilities. One person cannot possibly do justice to both jobs. Even though it is feasible for the college president to delegate to another substantially all of his tasks as a religious superior, one of the positions is bound to suffer. Even without the overload of responsibility, it seems at least questionable whether one and the same person would ordinarily have the requisite qualities for both positions. The qualifications of a good religious superior are not necessarily those of a good college president, and vice versa.

Moreover, when a college president is also superior of the Religious Community attached to the college, he is limited by Church law in his tenure as a religious superior to not more than two three-year terms. As a college president only, it is possible to have indefinite tenure. Nowadays it takes five or six years for a college president to get to be known, to find his way around in educational circles, and to have any influence outside his own institution. Under a maximum tenure of six years, he no sooner begins to be known and to know others than he is replaced, probably by an unknown who must begin all over again. This practice prevents a college president from having any influence outside his own institution. The constant turnover of presidents gives the appearance of instability and tends to create an unfavorable impression of Catholic higher education. The separation of the offices of college president and religious superior will not automatically solve the problem of influence and representation, but it will make it possible for a president to become better known in educational circles and to take a more active part in state and national educational associations. When this occurs, it is good for the institution which the president represents because it broadens his experience and knowledge; and it is also good for Catholic education.

SEPARATION OF OFFICES

The policy of separating the college presidency from the office of local religious superior is now widely observed and has proved to be satisfactory in most instances. In some colleges it works smoothly and satisfactorily. In other instances it does not work satisfactorily, chiefly because of the failure to make a proper separation of the functions of the two offices and to select compatible officials. In general, it would seem that Religious Communities of men have adjusted themselves more readily to this situation than Religious Communities of women.

In separating the offices of president and religious superior, it is a great mistake and a definite handicap to a college to retain officially in the hand of the religious superior any functions that are regularly exercised by college presidents. As administrative head of the college, the president must have charge of the preparation of the budget, the control of expenditures, the work of planning, the over-all supervision of plant and maintenance, and the like. If, for example, the office of college treasurer or business manager was joined formally with the office of religious superior, great difficulty might be created. This does not mean necessarily that a religious superior who has the time, the ability, and the willingness, should not perform certain college functions, whether of teaching or administration. But the superior should perform these functions as a member of the college staff responsible to the president, and not as religious superior.

Usually where there is a smoothly working relationship between the college president and the religious superior, it will be found that there have been established definite norms for their guidance. Areas of responsibility have been clearly marked out, respective duties have been defined, a procedure for settling problems of debatable jurisdiction has been worked out, and all this may even have been drawn up in writing with the approval of the major superior—a procedure very important and desirable in all cases where separation is planned or has been effected.

In making the separation between the offices of college president and religious superior, the division of functions must be definite and clear-cut. The college president should have the same authority and responsibilities that are customarily attached to the presidency in other colleges. The religious superior has the responsibilities that go with the care of a Religious Community as distinct from the college entity. Individual Religious in the college community should be given to understand that they have a twofold responsibility. In those matters which pertain to their personal and religious life, they are responsible to the religious superior; in all that pertains to their duties in the college, they are responsible to the college president, in the same way as lay members of the staff or religious teachers who happen to be members of another Religious Community.

It is surprising that the constitutions of Religious Communities do not generally make specific provision for the authority which must be invested in the heads of educational institutions conducted by Religious in this country. Although there seems to be no question that the problem can be worked out satisfactorily by provincial superiors,[1] it will probably not have the desired definiteness and stability until it is given constitutional recognition.[2]

STATUS FOR RELIGIOUS SUPERIOR

To say that there is no place in the operation of the college for the local superior as such, does not mean that a position of honorable status in the college cannot and should not be found for the one who is the religious superior. If he or she is isolated completely from the college, an embarrassing, if not untenable, position might be created for a religious superior.

If a religious superior wishes to serve as a faculty member or as a subordinate administrator in the college, this would confer college status. Membership on the board of trustees would, of course, confer prominent and honorable status in the college without direct involvement in operation. This is the chief reason why the author advocates that the local religious superior ought to be the ex officio vice chairman of the board of trustees.[3] The religious superior is assured thereby an honorable title and place at all college functions. Thus a religious superior could appear at college functions either as a trustee, an administrative officer, or as a faculty member, depending upon which of these roles may be held, but not as a religious superior.

In looking after the needs of the Religious family the local religious superior, like the head of any family, should have responsible dominion in the home and should have control of the funds necessary to provide for the needs of the family. To this end it is important to have a Community fund, completely separate from college funds and under the jurisdiction of the local religious

[1] This has reference to Religious Communities which have an international headquarters but are organized on a national basis with one or more separate provinces.

[2] The Constitution of a Religious Community for men which makes specific provision for separating the office of head of a school from the office of the local religious superior, provides that:
"The head of the school shall have power and authority over all that pertains to the operation of the school. Both teachers and students are bound to obey him in all that pertains to his office."

[3] In Benedictine Communities the major superior is usually also the local superior and, in this case, would be the chairman of the board rather than vice chairman.

superior. Out of this fund all Community expenses and all personal expenses of the Religious are cared for. A separate residence for the Religious Community, that is not a part of other college buildings, is also an important element in protecting the independence and status of the local superior.

NEED FOR TEAMWORK

The separation of responsibilities will not work smoothly in practice unless the two persons, the local religious superior and the college president, are picked as a team and not as individuals. The local religious superior has to be one who is content to stay in the background, to attend strictly to the affairs of the Religious Community, permitting the college president to run the educational institution, to occupy the center of the stage, and to take all the bows. Since both must deal with the same members of the Religious Community, they must work closely together, co-ordinating their activities so as to avoid any occasion for friction. It is, of course, most important that the college president, as a member of the Religious Community, recognizes the position of the superior and shows personally every respect and courtesy to the religious superior. The president should make certain, as far as possible, that all members of the staff of the college observe similar courtesy and respect for the religious superior.

Where an ideal relationship exists, as it should and can, the local superior will be the unseen benefactor who contributes greatly to the success of the college by looking after the personal needs and spiritual welfare of all the members of the Religious Community, keeping them reasonably happy and content, and encouraging and supporting the work of the college president.

CHAPTER 6

Presidential Relationships

ALTHOUGH IT may be too much to say that a college president can make or break his college, there is no doubt that he can do much to help or to hinder its progress. To a large extent he can influence the smooth operation of the college through his personal tact in dealing with others, whether within the institution itself or outside. It would not be possible, of course, to deal even superficially with all these relations, because one college differs from another. But we can consider briefly some internal and external relationships which are common to most presidents of Catholic colleges.

INTERNAL RELATIONS

There is very little difference in the broad category of internal relationships which confront most college presidents, although details may differ greatly from institution to institution, depending on many variable factors.

Relations with the Board of Trustees: A Board of Trustees can be extremely helpful, it may be little more than a legal front, or it can become very meddlesome in the internal affairs of the college. A lot will depend upon the prudence, tact, and resourcefulness of the president, plus the interest which he arouses in the board, the confidence which he inspires in his administration of the college, the clarity of his reports, and the logic and reasonable-

49

ness with which he presents his various requests to the board. In most Catholic colleges members of the Religious Community comprise a majority of the board, with the major superior as the presiding officer. Such a board will have considerable influence with the Religious attached to the college and can greatly assist the president through its support. This presupposes that the board meets regularly and frequently, and that the president makes use of these meetings to keep the board (including the major superior) fully informed of the problems which confront the college.

Relations with Administrative Officers: No college worthy of the name can afford to be a one-man show. The president must have associated with him other administrative officers who have well-defined functions and responsibilities. These officers ought to be free to carry out their duties within the general policies approved by the president. He should always be available to them for consultation and advice when requested.

It is the president's responsibility to see that subordinates carry out their duties efficiently. They should have his unwavering moral support when they require it, but he should not interfere or go over their heads without serious reason. This presupposes, of course, that an administrative officer recognizes that his responsibilities and authority are delegated, that he should keep his immediate superior informed of all important activities and consult with him whenever it seems prudent or advisable.

The admissions office, for example, should be governed by well-defined policies. In denying admission to students within these established policies, the admissions officer should have the full support of the president when outside or inside pressures arise. Parents or alumni may appeal from a decision of the admissions office directly to the president, and they should be courteously received by him. If the case seems to warrant reconsideration, he should make no commitments then and there; he should discuss the whole problem with the admissions officer and they should agree what further action, if any, needs to be taken. Never should a president accept a student and then tell the admissions officer what he has done; much less should he order the acceptance of a student regardless of circumstances.

The authority of a college president is considerable, but not as absolute as it might be for the head of a large business or industrial undertaking. It is most effective when he strives for the consensus of his staff officials. There is also a difference between the authority and procedure of a college president and that of a religious superior who is accustomed to religious obedience. The difficulty of making a distinction between the types of authority proper to the two offices is another reason why both positions should not be held simultaneously by the same person.

Relations with the Faculty: One of the most delicate relationships of a college president is that with the faculty, individually and collectively, lay and Religious. At times he may require the patience of Job, at other times the wisdom of Solomon, at other times the tact of a seasoned diplomat. The reason for this is to be found in the unique character of the relationship, which differs radically from that of employer and employee. A professor is very conscious of the fact that he is not a hired hand, that his scholarship and effectiveness in the classroom cannot be brought about by orders from above. Except through encouragement and persuasion, the president's powers of action with faculty members are largely negative. He has the difficult job of trying to get all the members of the faculty to carry on the essential work of the institution without being able to compel any one of them. This is why the college presidency more than almost any other job calls for true leadership.

This does not mean that the college president is not called upon to make administrative decisions which may affect the faculty. A president with no decisions to make would be an anomaly. But understanding the sensitive relationship of his position, he will not make decisions hastily without weighing carefully all possible reactions or effects. Neither will he put off or delay necessary decisions without good reason. Nothing causes the morale of a college to deteriorate more rapidly than the college president who cannot make up his mind, who hesitates to make decisions in the hope that somehow or other matters will eventually work out satisfactorily, or the problem will disappear entirely.

It is a good thing for a president to be approachable both with administrators and faculty members. In some cases this may mean an "open-door" policy, where formal appointments are not necessary and the president is regularly available when not otherwise engaged. This will not prove burdensome if his administrative organization is well set up and if he tactfully makes it clear in the first few interviews that, while he will listen sympathetically, he will not bypass the authority of subordinate officials. A reputation for approachability can act as a safety valve in time of need.

Relations with Students: As colleges are now organized, the president will have few direct contacts with students, unless he goes out of his way to seek these contacts. It seems important that he should have his finger, so to speak, on the pulse of the student body. How to do this without running afoul of other administrative officers is a problem to be solved on each campus. A lot will depend on circumstances, on the character of the student body, and on the personality and wishes of the president.

Some presidents have found that the regular teaching of a class or two has enabled them to maintain helpful direct contacts with students. Other presidents have worked closely with student leaders through regular meetings and informal contacts. One president found that it helped to let students understand that his office door was open to them when he was not otherwise engaged. He claimed that his "open-door" policy made no heavy demands on his time because few students actually made use of the privilege; but the fact that students knew the door was open to them had a psychological value.

Other presidents have entertained student groups in their homes or have found that attendance at student socials, dinners, entertainments and the like, have furnished helpful student contacts. In most instances some form of regular and direct contact with student leaders offers the most practicable solution. Fortunately, at least in the smaller colleges, communication among students is so effective that a president's successful contacts with even small groups of students can have far-ranging good effects on all the students.[1]

Relations with Religious Community: The Religious Commu-

---

[1] *Letters to College Presidents* by Jones/Stanford/White (Englewood Cliffs, N.J.: Prentice-Hall, 1964); see Chapter 16, "Relationships with Students," for further sidelights on these relationships.

nity that operates a college is a very special "public," with which the president of the college must maintain good relations. This is particularly so if the Community is relatively small and operates a single college. Since the property of Religious Communities is held in common, the members of the Community are like stockholders in a business concern. There are no "dividends," of course, and their interest in the college is not financial, but it may be for that reason all the more vital and real. Frequently it is manifested in a subtle but clearly definable feeling that *this is our institution.* Very often these Religious have their own ideas as to how the institution ought to be run, even though they may never have been connected with the college either as faculty member or administrative officer.

There is an innate interest here among the members of the Religious Community that must be cultivated for the best interest of the college. All concerned must be kept fully informed, and their interest directed in beneficial ways. If this interest is misdirected, or if it is converted into apathy, the task of the president of the college is made more difficult. To communicate effectively with his fellow Religious and to inspire in them confidence in his administration is a real test of a president's abilities.

EXTERNAL RELATIONS

The chief work of the president off the college campus can be summed up under the heading of Public Relations. The importance of fostering good public relations for the college cannot be sufficiently emphasized. This is an area where the college president must be alert and active because, without intelligent leadership on his part, good public relations cannot be achieved. As the subject of public relations is a rather large one, we can comment here only briefly on the president's duties in regard to the local diocese, to alumni, to educational associations, to other national organizations, to sister institutions, and to the general public.

Relations with the Diocese: There are about a dozen Catholic colleges and universities, apart from diocesan seminaries, which are operated under the direction of the resident bishop. These are known as diocesan colleges. In a diocesan college, the diocese with its one or more bishops, its clergy and people comprise a very important "public" for the college. Here the president's relationships with the bishop, the clergy and the people of the diocese are more direct than those of the president of a college operated by a Religious Community. Ordinarily the resident bishop is the chairman of the governing board of the college. The diocesan clergy who serve the college are appointed by the bishop. Although there is more of a feeling of diocesan responsibility toward these colleges, they must operate financially, for the most part, on their own. It is apparent, therefore, that the president of a diocesan college must make every effort to cultivate good and harmonious relations with the head of the diocese and with the clergy and people of the diocese.

Colleges operated by Religious Communities are more independent of the diocese in which they are situated. At the time of foundation these colleges must have the approval or consent of the resident bishop. In giving this approval the bishop ordinarily accepts no financial responsibility for the college, nor does he enter into its management or operation. The resident bishop is responsible, however, for the purity of Catholic faith and morality within the confines of his ecclesiastical jurisdiction. If a college operated by a Religious Community were to depart from the teachings of the Church in matters of faith and morals, the bishop would have not only the right but the duty to step in and apply proper corrective measures. Instances of this kind are so rare that they are practically unknown in this country.

The interest, the encouragement and the assistance which an individual college receives from the bishop depends on many factors. Among these factors we can list such items as the following: the bishop's personal attitude toward the college and the Religious Community which operates the college; his personal relationships with the president of the college; his opinion as to whether or not the college is doing a worth-while educational job; his belief in the importance of the college to the educational work of the diocese; and other considerations of like nature. The president's task in cultivating and preserving good relations in the diocese is no less important in a college operated by a Religious

Community than it is in a diocesan college. In fact it may be more important.

Relations with Alumni: Good alumni relations are important for the president to maintain. Alumni are the product of the college. Their successes or their failures reflect back on their college. To some degree also, they can bask in the successes of their college or be embarrassed by its failures. Their interest and good will can be of great assistance to the college in many ways. But alumni interest cannot be taken for granted. It must be deliberately cultivated if it is to produce intelligent support.

No one can represent the college more effectively to alumni than the president. Therefore, he should make every effort to appear personally at least once a year before the various regional meetings, to greet and talk with alumni who visit the college. There have been times in the past when alumni interest and activity seemed to be more troublesome than helpful to a college, and some presidents have wondered whether it was really worth the time, the effort, and the inconvenience. Today there has been a revolution in alumni attitudes and alumni support of their colleges. Alumni have proven to be a very important arm of support for the college, both financially and otherwise.

In many Catholic colleges the president has the more or less delicate problem of integrating the alumni (or alumnae) office within the administrative setup of the college. This means that the alumni office, its personnel and its budget, are taken over as one of the activities of the college, like the admissions office or the registrar's office. This is the arrangement that is now successfully employed in most non-Catholic colleges, and is of considerable importance for the success of a well-organized development program.

Paradoxically enough, in the past many presidents of Catholic colleges encouraged their alumni organizations to take over the supervision and support of the alumni office in order that the colleges might be freed from the burden of support. In some instances this led to separate incorporation for the alumni association. It is not easy to reverse this process, to persuade such alumni groups to give up their seeming independence and to let the college take over the alumni office. But by giving up a little independence, they will gain far more in the prestige and effectiveness of the alumni organization. At the same time alumni must be convinced that it is their duty to contribute regularly to an annual alumni fund which goes directly into the current funds of the college.

Regarding this alumni relationship, presidents of Catholic colleges for women have the particular task of persuading their alumnae to put aside the snobbery which rules out from full membership in the alumnae association all those who have not formally graduated from the college. This is a policy which not even the most exclusive colleges would countenance today.

Relations with Educational Associations: Rightly or wrongly the prestige of a college, even its academic standing, is frequently judged by the reputation which its president has established in various educational associations. In the best interests of his institution a college president cannot afford to refrain from taking an active part in the chief educational associations. A program of minimum participation should include at least the Association of American Colleges,[2] American Council on Education, the College and University Department of the National Catholic Educational Association, the Regional Accrediting Association, and the appropriate State College Association. Although there has been a marked improvement in recent years, there are still some Catholic college executives who are not as active as they could be in the various educational associations.

Relations with other National Organizations: It would hardly be possible for a college president to keep in personal contact with the many national organizations which touch only particular phases of college administration. Nevertheless some of these organizations have such a helpful impact on college administration that a president cannot personally afford to ignore them or to leave representation entirely to other members of his staff.

The author has in mind particularly the American Alumni Council and the American College Public Relations Association, both of which maintain national headquarters in Washington, D.C. It is assumed, of course, that a college will maintain mem-

---

[2] Membership is open to all regionally accredited four-year colleges.

bership in these organizations, and that the appropriate staff officers will participate in the meetings and activities of these organizations. But it is well worth a president's time to keep personally informed by selective reading of their publications and by attending at least one of their national meetings.

The Council for Financial Aid to Education, Inc., with headquarters in New York City, is another organization whose bulletins and publications ought to receive more than cursory attention. This is a service organization, with no membership provisions, sponsored by business and industrial leaders with foundation support. It does not of itself raise or give away money, but it has had a tremendous influence in encouraging voluntary support for higher education.

Relations with Sister Institutions: There are certain fundamental courtesies that should mark all inter-college relationships, and that are particularly desirable in relationships with non-Catholic colleges, especially those that are church-related. To receive regularly invitations to special celebrations, inaugurations, centennials and so on, yet to acknowledge these seldom; to attend rarely, if at all, or to send unknown substitutes—all of this betrays a lack of fundamental courtesy which discourages cordial relations with sister institutions. There are those who consider that greater laxity in these fundamental courtesies is found among presidents of Catholic colleges than among presidents of other colleges.

There seems to be no question that an appreciable number of presidents of Catholic colleges are notably deficient in handling personal correspondence. Letters addressed personally to a president may be ignored entirely or, what is only a little less discourteous, may be answered by a subordinate officer. One educator maintains a file marked "blacklist of presidents." It contains a notable collection of carbon copies of letters, written from time to time to various Catholic college presidents, which never received the courtesy of an acknowledgement.

Neglect of correspondence is inexcusable on the part of presidents of colleges, who should show the way in good public relations. It is very difficult to understand this discourtesy, because most college presidents have competent secretaries who could take responsibility for seeing that correspondence is not neglected and that letters are answered without a great delay. With any encouragement at all, a secretary could prepare suitable acknowledgments for most of these letters, requiring only the president's signature.

Relations with the General Public: It is certainly desirable that a college have the esteem and respect of the general public. Of course this depends above all on the performance of the college as an educational institution, for which the president has a major share of responsibility. In addition, however, he can exercise a beneficial influence through his own contacts with the public. He will have frequent opportunities to appear in public, to speak to various groups and to lend his encouragement to various movements for the public good. All of these relationships must be dignified. It is not necessary for him to be an active Rotary or Lion's Club member, though he may occasionally speak before such groups. He must not become embroiled in doubtful movements or in partisan politics. There are many more helpful ways for him to employ his talents.

No one will question that it is a demanding responsibility which requires the college president to use wisely and well the multiple relationships of his office. But one who really makes the effort will find it a rewarding experience. Moreover, one who has had even moderate success in thus cultivating good public relations is more likely to be conscious of the importance of enlisting all members of the college family, from the youngest to the eldest, in a college-wide effort to build and maintain good public relations for the college.

CHAPTER 7

The Academic Dean

NEXT TO the president the most important administrative officer is the academic dean. At one time this official was known simply as "the Dean." But of late years even the smallest college has more than one dean so that it is now necessary to add a qualifying adjective.

We are concerned here only with the academic dean—"The Dean of the College"—who directs the educational activities which are the chief reason for the existence of the college. Usually and appropriately, at least in the small college, the dean is the second in command.

No one person in the college should be in a better position than the dean to understand the problems of students and faculty members. No one should be able to judge better than the dean the caliber of faculty members and the efficiency of their work in the classroom. No one should be able to appraise better the student body as a whole, and to decide whether there are weaknesses in admission procedures. For these reasons alone, the dean is the logical adviser to the president on all matters affecting faculty and students. On matters of educational policy it is the dean who should make recommendations to the president. The president would be rash indeed if he did not take the dean into his confidence and consult with him on all matters relating to the policies of the college.

RELATIONSHIPS OF THE DEAN

The various relationships of the dean in the day-to-day operation of the college require prudence and tact and considerable patience. It is not possible to describe in detail all these relationships, but the following outline gives some idea of the scope of the dean's responsibilities.

The dean's relations with the president ought to be close and cordial, with no secrets or reservations between them. If the dean functions as acting president in the absence of the president it is important that he be aware at least of the most important items of business which pass through the president's office. The dean must in turn apprise the president of what is going on in classrooms and laboratories and in the various activities of the campus, without bothering him with needless details. At times the president must be tactfully encouraged to make decisions on matters that cannot be postponed, without his being made aware that he is being goaded into action.

A prominent educator, who has had considerable experience in college visitations of one kind or another, once told the writer it has always bothered him to discover that major problems, though varying from institution to institution, are often rooted in the relationship between the president and the dean. "Sometimes," he said, "it was clear that the president did not trust nor rely on the dean. Sometimes it was equally clear that the dean did not trust the president and had difficulty in working with him. Frequently the antagonisms were mutual." Wherever such a situation exists, it is, of course, harmful to the college. Fortunate, therefore, is the college which has a president and a dean who have mutual confidence in each other and who work as a well-organized team.

Where there has been the customary delegation of authority corresponding with recognized areas of administration, there will be three or four college officials other than the dean who bear the distinction of reporting directly to the president. The chart of the administrative organization may represent these officials on the same level as the academic dean. But the bylaws of administration should make it clear that the dean is the first among equals;

and the president should insist that the privilege which certain officials have in reporting directly to him does not imply that they can by-pass the dean or that they need not work in close harmony with him. Sometimes the establishment of separate areas of administration creates touchy and delicate situations for the academic dean, even though he is the second in command. That is why I think it is a mistake in a moderate-sized college for any administrative officer other than the dean to be given the title of vice president.

The dean should have considerable influence in shaping curricula, courses, and methods of instruction, but, if he is a wise dean, he will make liberal use of faculty committees and heads of departments. The assignment and supervision of teachers, at least to the extent of seeing to it that equitable teaching loads are maintained, are matters with which the dean must be concerned, even though department heads handle the details. It will be the dean's task to know the strength and weakness of individual faculty members, and to have considerable influence in the renewal and termination of appointments and in the selection of new faculty members. The dean must ascertain whether teachers are attending classes regularly and promptly, and whether reasonable discipline in the classroom or laboratory is being maintained, without creating the impression that he (or she) is a "top sergeant." The dean can do much in smoothing internal relations by being patient with the conflicts and petty squabbles that sometimes arise between faculty members themselves or between faculty members and students. Frequently, for instance, the dean can prepare the way for a hesitant professor to speak to the president on a necessary matter, without letting the hesitant one know that he has done so.

Concern for the progress and academic welfare of students is a function of the dean, even in institutions where there is a well-developed system of student advisers. The responsibility for the classification and assignment of students to classes also belongs to the dean, even when most of the details are taken care of by a registrar or by department chairmen. The dean's contacts with the students can be an important asset in public relations if they are managed with tact and understanding, just as they can be a liability if they are brusque and autocratic. The dean's close relations with students will frequently bring him into contact, either in person or by letter, with the parents of students. There is an opportunity here to make a significant contribution to good public relations for the college.

STUDENT OF HIGHER EDUCATION

The dean must always be a student of higher education and should be familiar with what is going on academically in other colleges and universities. He should know what are the requirements of graduate schools, what are the chief developments in educational thought and practice. Sometimes the dean will be expected to be the academic mentor of the president, particularly on what may be called the "technical" matters of education—such things as tests and measurements, the validity of evaluative criteria, and the like. But heaven help the dean who has to try to make up for the lack of executive ability in the president!

The dean should be frequently in attendance at appropriate educational meetings even when the president attends. This is particularly the case with the meetings of the regional accrediting association and of state and local groups. In fact the dean should be sufficiently abreast of what is current in the various educational associations so that at any time he can serve as the official representative of the college in the absence of the president.

EDUCATIONAL LEADER

The dean must find time to do imaginative and constructive thinking about the college, its objectives and its curriculum. Unless he is able to delegate responsibilities to others he will not have time to do this, because he will get bogged down with details that others could handle just as well. If the dean wishes to exercise leadership among his faculty, he must always resist the temptation to have things done through his office merely because that is the easiest and quickest way to get a task done. The time and effort would be better expended if he could see to it tactfully that the job is done by the one who ought to do it.

LIGHTENING THE LOAD

It sometimes happens that when the president is under pressure to divest himself of some of the details of his office in order to give more time, for example, to development work, what he gives up is passed on directly or indirectly to the dean. This may serve to complicate the problems of an already overburdened dean. In such instances there is no panacea that will effectively relieve the dean of an overload of details and responsibilities. But methods and techniques that have been found helpful in some colleges may at least have suggestive value for others.

It is a great advantage to the dean if the faculty is organized into a reasonably small number of compact departments, each headed by an active chairman who reports to the dean. If this type of organization really functions as described in Chapter 10, it will not only relieve the dean of endless details but will make his contacts with department chairmen and faculty members more effective and efficient.

The dean should not hesitate to co-opt a faculty member who has particular ability in a special field. For example, it still frequently happens that the dean has the responsibility of making up class schedules. As anyone in administration knows, schedule-making is an art that requires peculiar perspicacity, especially if courses are relatively numerous, classroom space and faculty members limited, and student programs irregular—a not unusual combination. In planning a schedule of classes so as to avoid as many conflicts as possible and keep everyone reasonably satisfied, the dean has a problem similar to that of trying to solve a complicated jigsaw puzzle while playing a checker game against a clever opponent.

In this situation one dean was fortunate enough to find a chemistry professor who had a passion for working on such problems and preferred them to crossword puzzles. The professor took great pride in this undertaking and showed up regularly at schedule-making time without any need of a reminder. Between them, the two were able to develop ingenious devices in the form of wall charts where, with the liberal use of movable pieces of colored cardboard, they were able to see at a glance, to study and to ponder, without the necessity of endlessly thumbing through schedule cards in order to check possible conflicts or to make better adjustments. Today, of course, with electronic data-processing the problem of schedules is handled in the larger institutions, if not with more humanity, at least with more dispatch and, probably, efficiency.

It would be helpful for the dean and it would be a service to the Religious Community, if a young Religious who seems to have administrative promise could be co-opted by the dean to serve as an understudy, as described in Chapter 9. This is a three-way proposition: the dean can have some assistance, the young Religious can be given an insight into college administration and, hopefully, the Religious Community will have an addition to the pool of administrative personnel.

UNSELFISH SERVICE

There is nothing spectacular about the office of academic dean; the occupant will seldom figure in newspaper publicity or be acclaimed by alumni or the general public. College deans have a way of gracefully living on and dying in harness, or retiring with dignity at as ripe an age as college regulations will permit. Perhaps it is to be regretted that college presidents seldom pass through the chastening fires of a deanship. If there is an unsung hero in the college, the chances are that it is the dean. All the more credit then, to the faithful, conscientious, untiring dean, who labors day in and day out both for the best interests of the students and for the continual improvement of the academic standing of the college.

CHAPTER 8

Administrative Organization

GOOD ADMINISTRATION has become more and more important as college operations have increased in complexity and expense. A poorly administered college is bound to suffer both financially and academically. Without efficient management a college can be internally wasteful of its resources, or extend services beyond its present or prospective means, and be in deep trouble both economically and educationally almost before realizing it. To assure good administration there is no substitute, of course, for an able and knowledgeable chief administrator as President of the college. But a college is not a one-man institution. A President must have competent assistants and good organization.

SHARING RESPONSIBILITY

The President bears the responsibility for the operation of the entire institution, but it does not follow that he will perform all the administrative functions himself. The administration of a college is so complex that efficient operation requires a wide delegation of power and responsibility to others. Frequently there is difficulty here. Either the President seems unwilling to delegate responsibility, or those who accept delegated responsibility seem unwilling to recognize the President's primary responsibility for unified executive direction.

One who bears full responsibility for any undertaking can never quite divest himself of that responsibility, even by delegating it to another. Therefore, the successful delegation of responsibility requires harmonious relationships between President and staff members. The one who delegates responsibility must be aware of what is being done by his staff members, without ever seeming to distrust them or to interfere with the activities in their charge. The one who accepts the delegation of responsibility must keep his superior fully informed, without seeming to be excessively dependent upon him and without bothering him with unimportant details.

Areas of Administration

There are today five distinct areas of administration which should be common to Catholic colleges of moderate size. The central and most important area is concerned with the academic welfare or intellectual interests of students. This area is the province of the Academic Dean. In looking after the academic welfare of the students the Dean must of necessity direct and guide the faculty, which is engaged in providing academic leadership in the various fields of learning.

Then there are the non-academic interests of students, the so-called "student personnel services" which have to do with the physical, social, and recreational needs of students. In recent years there has been a great expansion of these services. This expansion involves extensive extracurricular activities and certain auxiliary enterprises. The coordination and supervision of this area is the province of an administrator whom we will designate "Director of Student Affairs." This administrator is also known variously as Director of Student Personnel Services, Director of Students, Dean of Students, Vice President for Student Affairs, and so on.

There is also the spiritual welfare of students. The concern here is to provide the students with appropriate religious services and devotions, periodic spiritual retreats, opportunities for spiritual counseling, and encouragement and guidance for group religious activities. (Actual courses in theology or religion are included under academic affairs.) In many ways this spiritual area is the least complicated in college administration and requires far less administrative personnel. Probably this is why some colleges list the Chaplain under student personnel services. But logically and psychologically he should not be grouped with all the heterogeneous activities to be found in a student personnel program. He should be given the prestige of a top echelon administrator and have opportunity for direct access to the President, even though most of his relationships will be with the Academic Dean and the Director of Student Affairs. Ordinarily, however, there is no necessity for him to be a member of the President's Administrative Council mentioned below.

Fourth, there is the business and financial area, which is the province of the Business Manager or Treasurer, or whatever title may be used. In this area of administration are handled such mundane matters as the management of the financial affairs of the college, the collection of revenue, the purchase of equipment and supplies, the payment of bills, the maintenance of buildings, grounds and equipment, the management of auxiliary enterprises, the welfare of non-academic personnel, and so on. Although this area is only indirectly connected with man's intellectual life, it is nonetheless important. Without business and financial management of a high order, a college could hardly operate today.

Finally, there is the most recent specialized field in college administration, the so-called "development and public relations" area. This embraces all public relations activities. It should include, or at least co-ordinate, alumni activities, especially those that have to do with alumni public relations and alumni fund raising. It should control or co-ordinate all fund-raising activities of whatever nature. It does not touch, of course, the regular or earned income of a college. Rather it seeks to supplement this income by the continuous, systematic tapping of various sources of voluntary giving. The administrator who heads this program goes by various titles, such as Director of Development, Director of University Relations, Vice President for Development, and so on. For our purpose we will use the more expressive title, Director of Development and Public Relations.

The five areas of administration which have been briefly described ought to be in charge of five competent administrators under the President, bearing the following or equivalent titles: the Dean, the Director of Student Affairs, the Chaplain, the Treasurer-Business Manager, and the Director of Development and Public Relations. These officers are in a sense co-equals, because they head the chief areas of administration and each reports directly to the President. But the Dean, who directs the academic program and is second in command under the President, takes precedence.

ADMINISTRATIVE COUNCIL

It is very important that these officers shall be in constant communication with the President and with one another. There is danger that each may become so intent on managing his own area of administration that he may ignore the others, and may even neglect to keep the President informed as to what is going on in his area. One way to avoid this danger is through an Administrative Council. This Council is composed of the heads of the four more complex areas of administration under the President as chairman. The chaplain is not ordinarily included, but he can be invited to meetings whenever matters to be discussed are within his special area of responsibility.

One of the prime purposes of the Administrative Council is to provide frequent opportunity for communication between the heads of the various areas of administration. This is the place for difficulties to be shared, for disagreements to be aired, and for cooperation to be enlisted. For that reason one of the first items of business at every meeting of the Council should be brief reports from each of the four administrative areas. The Council also serves in an important advisory capacity to the President, and gives consideration especially to such matters as he may present to it. In many colleges this Council meets at the beginning of every week during the school year.

The writer does not believe that subordinate administrators or faculty members should be members of this Council because of its specific purposes just mentioned. But there are occasions when non-members should be invited to meetings of the Council, especially when matters directly touching on their responsibilities are being considered. Each head of an administrative area, however, should hold frequent meetings of his own staff to ensure efficient communication.

FLEXIBILITY OF ORGANIZATION

In building an administrative organization it would be ideal if one could work it out along sound lines, knowing that one had the necessary people to fill the various posts or could readily obtain them. Unfortunately this is seldom the case. There are many reasons, financial and otherwise, which make it necessary to temper idealism, adjust to the situation at hand, and do the best that one can under the circumstances. If one must select personnel from the religious order which operates the college, the chances are that the pool from which one may draw administrators will be very small. Even if one has the opportunity to select lay personnel one will be limited, nevertheless, by the financial rewards one can offer.

The organization of even the smallest college should be based on a clear division of administrative functions—such as the five areas suggested above—even though it cannot immediately be reflected in staff positions. Two areas of responsibility may have to be temporarily covered by the occupant of a single post. For the time being it may be necessary for the President to serve as Director of Development, or for the Dean to serve as Director of Student Affairs. As the college develops and personnel are obtainable, the proper separation of positions can be made definitely and painlessly. For a similar reason, recognition of the different offices of the Registrar and the Director of Admissions is to be recommended, even though the size of the college at this time does not warrant their separation and one person can readily handle the functions of both offices. If a college will make these distinctions in both organizational chart and bylaws, its organization will be flexible enough to provide for future growth without essential modifications.

MULTIPLICATION OF TITLES

The multiplication of titles, however necessary, is not without its hazards. This can be learned from the experience of the larger institutions of higher learning. Thus the college of moderate size should be wary of the multiplication of deans and vice presidents. This does not imply that responsibility should not be shared. Quite the contrary! However, responsibility can be shared and authority divided without employing university titles. Less imposing titles can be used. A situation in which there are all generals and no lieutenants or corporals is not healthy.

ORGANIZATIONAL CHART AND BYLAWS

If there is to be order and system in the administration of a college, delegation of responsibility must be carefully planned and executed. There must be no vagueness or uncertainty on the part of the one delegating responsibility, or on the part of the one accepting the responsibility. There are two administrative devices that will help to dispel vagueness and uncertainty: namely, an organizational chart and a set of bylaws. The organizational chart is designed to give visual representation to the manner in which responsibility and authority are delegated. But this is not enough. There must be a written *modus operandi* that spells out in greater detail the responsibility and authority of the chief executive and the major and subordinate officials. This is the purpose of the bylaws of a college, which complement the organizational chart and make it functional.

There can be no standard chart of organization which will meet the needs of all colleges. But certain principles of organization apply to all or most institutions, and certain patterns of organization ought to apply to colleges of comparable size and complexity. This is particularly true of certain areas of administration which have become more and more specialized. (We are concerned here chiefly with the college of moderate size whose full-time enrollment does not exceed two thousand students, although much of what is said may apply also to larger colleges.)

The Organizational Chart

The diagramming of the administrative system of a college as it currently operates is the first requisite for making a study of its adequacy. Such a diagram or chart ought to show how the lines of communication and authority are laid down. It will reveal, for example, whether there are too many people reporting directly to the President, whether the Dean has too many irons in the fire, whether there is an equitable division of responsibility and authority. It may show that some officers have responsibilities not fully consonant with their positions.

An organizational chart is somewhat similar to the diagram of an English sentence, which identifies subject and predicate and then shows the relationship and dependency of the other words and phrases in the sentence. The organizational chart of a college should indicate, first of all, the dependency of the President on the board of trustees. Then it should show the dependency of the various other officers on the President. Not more than four or five of these officers normally report directly to the President. These are the top echelon officers, and all other staff members are under the immediate jurisdiction of one of them as indicated on the chart. If the previously mentioned areas of administration headed by five principal officers under the President are accepted, this will provide five main divisions for the organizational chart. With this as a basis, the proper allocation of functions and officers can readily be worked out in orderly fashion.

An orderly organizational chart will help to preserve balance in establishing a new office. Thus, if the trustees believe that a Vice-Presidency should be established and combined with the duties of another office, an organizational chart should make it evident that the title ought to be given to the College Dean, who is considered to be second in command to the President. In this instance he would have the title "Vice President and Dean" or "Vice President for Academic Affairs." Although it may be questioned whether a college of moderate enrollment has need, ordinarily, for even a part-time Vice President, if the circumstances in a particular college are such as to require the services of a full-time Vice President, this need not create any disorganization in chart or bylaws. The new officer, as second in command to the President, would be interposed on the chart between the President and the Academic Dean. Presumably, in addition to the ordinary standby functions of a Vice President, he would also be assigned special duties by the President.

If, despite the hazards mentioned, it be judged necessary or advantageous to have two or more vice presidents, the chart of organization would indicate that the following order in creating new vice presidents would be appropriate: after the Academic Vice President, the director of development could become "Vice President for Development"; the treasurer-business manager could become "Vice President for Business and Financial Affairs"; and finally the director of student affairs could become "Vice President for Student Affairs." This is not intended to suggest that a college of moderate enrollment needs even one vice president, but merely to illustrate flexibility in an organizational chart.

A SAMPLE CHART

The specimen chart which follows is more or less a "master" chart. It distinguishes the various areas of administration and allocates to each area the functions and responsibilities proper to it. It indicates that only five officials are expected to report directly to the President. All other officials and faculty members are responsible directly or indirectly to one of these five officials. There is not always complete agreement among educators as to where certain functions should be allocated. Thus some authorities would allocate the Registrar and Director of Admissions to the personnel area under the Director of Student Affairs. But the author believes that this pertains to the Academic Dean because the academic interest is paramount. Others would allocate student recruitment to the Development and Public Relations column. But the author believes that there is both an academic and a public relations interest here, and would list this in both columns and clarify the relationship in the bylaws.

This master chart should ordinarily be sufficient for a small college. For a larger college it is possible to work out a more detailed

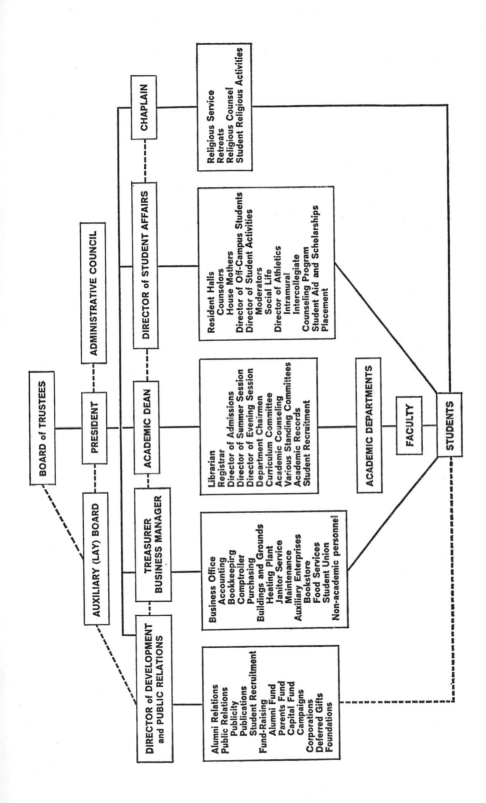

BOARD of TRUSTEES

ADMINISTRATIVE COUNCIL

PRESIDENT

AUXILIARY (LAY) BOARD

CHAPLAIN

DIRECTOR of STUDENT AFFAIRS

ACADEMIC DEAN

TREASURER
BUSINESS MANAGER

DIRECTOR of DEVELOPMENT
and PUBLIC RELATIONS

Religious Service
Retreats
Religious Counsel
Student Religious Activities

Resident Halls
Counselors
House Mothers
Director of Off-Campus Students
Director of Student Activities
Moderators
Social Life
Director of Athletics
Intramural
Intercollegiate
Counseling Program
Student Aid and Scholarships
Placement

Librarian
Registrar
Director of Admissions
Director of Summer Session
Director of Evening Session
Department Chairmen
Curriculum Committee
Academic Counseling
Various Standing Committees
Academic Records
Student Recruitment

Business Office
Accounting
Bookkeeping
Comptroller
Purchasing
Buildings and Grounds
Heating Plant
Janitor Service
Maintenance
Auxiliary Enterprises
Bookstore
Food Services
Student Union
Non-academic personnel

Alumni Relations
Public Relations
Publicity
Publications
Student Recruitment
Fund-Raising
Alumni Fund
Parents Fund
Capital Fund
Campaigns
Corporations
Deferred Gifts
Foundations

ACADEMIC DEPARTMENTS

FACULTY

STUDENTS

chart from the master chart, or better still, detailed charts for the separate areas of administration. In this way each member of the organization will know to whom he is expected to report. Two suggested samples are given in APPENDIX III for the academic administration and for the administration of student affairs. Similar charts, if desired, can be worked out for the remaining areas of administration and for any subdivisions, such as the library.

BYLAWS OF ADMINISTRATION

An organizational chart is only part of the effort needed to lay the groundwork for efficient administration. The chart must be complemented with bylaws, a written document which regulates the internal affairs of the college and spells out the duties of the various major and minor officials.

In listing the functions of the various administrative heads, it should be made clear that the Academic Dean is next in authority to the President; and heads of administrative areas must work in close co-operation with him, even though they are in direct contact with the President. Likewise, in listing the functions of the various staff officers, it would be well to mention to whom that particular staff officer is directly responsible, before mentioning specific duties. The cross relationships of certain staff officers and the necessity of close collaboration should also be mentioned.

Through the bylaws it is important to make clear just what are the duties and responsibilities of each participant in the administration of a college. Therefore, the clarity of the bylaws is of prime importance and should largely determine the style and format. This does not mean that all duties and responsibilities must be enumerated in great detail. It is desirable that the bylaws be flexible and streamlined as much as possible. This can be accomplished, while safeguarding clarity, by first defining briefly the scope of each office or position and then, by way of illustration, enumerating the chief duties or responsibilities of the office. Furthermore, the bylaws should be a model of simplicity by keeping sections and subsections to a minimum.

CONTENT OF BYLAWS

Bylaws of administration should include the following information set down appropriately in a series of numbered articles.

1. The legal name of the college.
2. A very brief statement of the purposes of the college.
3. Brief mention of the board of trustees, with number of members and general statement of the powers and duties of the board.[1]
4. Brief mention of the associate board, with number of members and general statement of the duties of the board.[1]
5. A series of articles enumerating briefly the functions and duties of the various officers of administration mentioned on the organizational chart, beginning with the president and ending, perhaps, with the departmental chairmen.
6. A series of articles dealing with the various standing committees of the faculty—the members, how designated and for what terms. Mention of *ad hoc* committees would also be appropriate.
7. The procedure for amending the bylaws at any meeting of the board of trustees, when proposed, with proper advance notice, by the president of the college.

BYLAWS ARE FOR USE

Once prepared, bylaws should receive the approval of the board of trustees and be put into effect. They will not be worth the paper they are written on, if they are filed away in a folder to be produced only when some visiting educator asks, "Do you have bylaws?" To be of any real value bylaws must be known and be followed strictly. As circumstances and conditions require, they may be amended and brought up to date.

The author does not favor printing the bylaws in the faculty handbook. This tends to clutter up the handbook with information that is not of frequent use to faculty members and to overshadow material that is relatively more important in the handbook. Duplicated copies of the complete bylaws should be made

---

[1] This assumes that there will be separate bylaws for the board of trustees and also for the associate board.

available, however, to all faculty members who wish copies. This could be noted in the faculty handbook, together with information as to where copies may be obtained. Each member of the administrative staff who is specifically mentioned in the bylaws should be sent a personal copy, with pages marked that pertain particularly to him.

WHY STATUTES?

It is sometimes suggested that a college ought to have both "statutes" and "bylaws." The reason advanced for this suggestion seems to be that "statutes" (the word "constitution" is sometimes used) set forth the governing rules of the institution in general terms only and should be relatively permanent, whereas "bylaws" go into more detail and are subject to more frequent revision. But the author can see no need for two such overlapping documents in the administration of an American college. There are practical reasons to substantiate this.

The Articles of Incorporation of some colleges are so detailed as to be equivalent to statutes. These colleges certainly have no need for statutes. Even colleges with very brief and general charters do not need both statutes and bylaws to regulate their affairs. If there are two such documents, there will be considerable repetition of text matter, but neither document will tell the whole story by itself. This doubles the amount of reading and tends to discourage regular use. Contradictions readily creep in if both documents are not simultaneously revised—not always an easy task because each will have its own procedure for revision, usually by different authorities. As a consequence it frequently happens that both documents are filed away for future revision against the next visit of an accrediting group. Presupposing that a college has separate bylaws for its Board of Trustees, the only other document required is a set of "Bylaws of Administration" for the college. Sample sets of both types of these bylaws may be found in APPENDIX II and APPENDIX IV.

A Memorandum

In earlier chapters it has been emphasized that a Catholic college has a two-fold character. It is chartered or incorporated by the State as an educational institution with legal status. It has a religious character in so far as it is conducted under the auspices of a Catholic Religious Community, Congregation or diocese of the Church, and upholds and teaches a Christian philosophy and way of life.

It is important to keep this distinction in mind. The bylaws we have been discussing are the civil bylaws of the college. They do not supplant or interfere with the provisions of the constitutions of a Religious Community or the provisions of the Canon Law of the Church. There is consequently no reason why any reference should be made in the civil bylaws to the Religious Community as such, or to its Rule and Constitutions, or to Canon Law.

CHAPTER 9

Filling Administrative Posts

ADMINISTRATIVE EFFICIENCY in colleges would be better served if it were always possible to fill a vacancy with a person who had been trained for the post or who came to it with previous administrative experience. The problem of finding capable administrators is not limited to Catholic colleges, but it can be more acute in colleges operated by a diocese or a Religious Community. When a non-Catholic college needs administrative personnel—a president, dean, registrar or treasurer, for example—it can usually shop around the country until, within budget limitations, it finds the person it wants. When a Catholic college needs a top executive, the procedure is much the same if the position is to be filled by a layman; but it is likely to be quite different when a Religious is wanted. Here the pool of available talent is confined largely to members of the Religious Community which operates the college. If there is no one available with the desired administrative experience, some one may be chosen for the position who not only has had no previous experience or preparation but may even lack the basic talent for administration.

Bad as this hit-or-miss system was in the past, when administrative posts were less complicated and specialized, it is now indefensible. The internal management of a Catholic college requires experienced executives. A college cannot afford to limp along until a president, a dean, or a business manager learns his job by profiting from his own mistakes.

Religious and Lay Administrators

Very few, if any, Catholic colleges today have prejudices about appointing competent laymen to top administrative posts. Particularly is this true when laymen make up a sizable share of the faculty. But in the average college operated by a Religious Community there is more involved than possible prejudice. A substantial salary must be paid to a layman as an administrator; whereas if a Religious competent to fill such a post were available, most of the salary involved would be contributed to the college. Also, it seems only proper that in a college sponsored and largely supported by a Religious Community, at least a fair number of those occupying top administrative posts should be Religious personnel. A balance must be struck in the number of administrative posts held by Religious and by laymen. But this balance will not be judiciously maintained unless Religious Communities *establish definite policies for the training of young Religious as future administrators.*

Discovering Administrative Talent

A good administrator must have some native ability and some experience in administration. Not everyone has innate administrative ability. It is difficult to be very specific about the qualities to look for in a *prospective* college administrator. Somebody once said that administration requires "inspired common sense." Certainly administrators in the higher echelon ought to have the ability to plan, to initiate, to consult, to delegate authority wisely, to work with others, to get others to work together, and to coordinate their efforts in the varied interests of the college. In a prospective administrator this implies a certain amount of prudence, tact and, at least, freedom from such personality traits as would prevent or inhibit these activities. Frequently an administrator has to deal with several matters at the same time or in rapid succession. This would indicate that a prospective administrator ought to be one who does not readily become flustered or confused under pressure. But in the final analysis you cannot be sure that a person has or does not have administrative ability by simply estimating his personality and character traits or making a judgment on the basis of his academic degrees. Actual trial is the only way to find out for certain.[1] But one cannot risk such a trial in an important assignment. In days when colleges were smaller and less complex, Religious faculty members, in the ordinary course of routine duties, had more chance of picking up administrative experience than exists in these days of complex colleges and more highly specialized administrative positions. Informal experience could be gained and native ability could be more readily observed. Today administrative experience in college has to be planned for.

A well known management consultant, with considerable experience in college surveys, has pointed out that today "the job of managing a college or university is more difficult and complex than the task of running a business of comparative size."[2] "But unlike industry," he says, "educational institutions have been slow to take steps to develop and train administrative talent."[3] He also remarks that "it is not unusual to find a college or university with important administrative positions to be filled and without qualified persons to fill them."[4]

Catholic colleges are no exception to this observation. If the task of finding and developing competent administrators is a critical need in colleges and universities which presumably can go anywhere to find their man, it is even more critical in Catholic colleges which expect to find administrators among the members of a particular Religious Community. Often the preparation and training of future administrators is completely overlooked, although for the most part it could be provided without any direct expense either at the home college or at another college, particularly one sponsored by the same Religious Community.

---

[1] Supported by a grant of $4,750,000 from the Ford Foundation, the American Council on Education is to begin in 1965 a 5-year program to provide year-long "on-the-job" internships, together with related educational experiences, to train promising young administrators for colleges and universities.

[2] Harlow J. Heneman (partner, Cresap, McCormick and Paget, Management Consultants), *Financing Higher Education 1960-70* (New York: McGraw-Hill, 1959); writing on "Opportunities for Better Institutional Management," p. 121.

[3] *Ibid.*, p. 129.

[4] *Ibid.*, p. 129.

Developing Administrative Talent

The best way to discover administrative talent is to select young Religious—as soon as they have attained a Master's degree and before they have gone very deeply into graduate studies, and *try them out* as understudies or assistants with experienced administrators. One who is being considered for administrative work would not be helped by a doctor's degree, for example, in educational administration, if he has no talent or ability for administration. On the other hand, an inspired teacher who has a doctorate in some academic or scientific field might make an excellent administrator, even though in a college understaffed with doctorates on the teaching faculty it is to be regretted that he may have to be put to administrative work.

One who is being tested for administrative aptitude should be definitely considered on trial with no assurance, implied or otherwise, that he is destined for an administrative office. On-the-job training can be combined, at least in the beginning, with a regular schedule of teaching assignments. Thus, for example, a young Religious can be taken into the president's office (or the dean's or the registrar's office) on an informal basis. Because of the tentative nature of the assignment, if not for more subtle psychological reasons, titles should be avoided altogether or toned down considerably. If a title must be used let it be "administrative assistant" in small letters rather than "Assistant to the President." The duties in the president's office could consist at first of miscellaneous tasks, such as arranging the details for a dinner, a lecture, or a concert, or collecting and preparing the information for a questionnaire or a report to be filed with some outside agency. If the handling of such assignments reveals talent and resourcefulness, more difficult tasks can be given. Meanwhile there is opportunity for the administrator to share information about routine duties, about problems that arise and the reasons why certain decisions are made.

For the young Religious who has the requisite personality, attitude and motivation such an experience could be valuable training for later administrative responsibility. If he has shown definite administrative aptitude there may be good reason why his further graduate training should be along practical administrative lines rather than directed toward a complete academic program.

The experienced administrative officer who gives time and effort to the training of an understudy should find it a rewarding experience. At the same time he will be making an investment for the Religious Community. Not only will the cause of better administration be served, but there will be a more fruitful accumulation of experience and a greater continuity of policy and practice in the administration of the college.

ADVANCING THE BEGINNER

It would not always be practicable, of course, to prepare young Religious for specific administrative posts, nor is this necessary. The chief purpose of a training program is to identify those who have administrative talent. When individuals have demonstrated this talent, it is to be hoped that they can be assigned to lower-echelon posts as the opportunity presents itself. As one of them gains experience and grows in competence, he can be advanced in responsibility as the need arises. It sometimes happens that an individual may be competent enough in administering an office where responsibility is more or less routine and where one task can be tackled singly before moving on to the next; but that same person would be completely ineffective in a more complex situation. This is the reason why neither seniority nor academic degrees can be the ruling consideration in advancing a person to an office involving greater responsibility. Only the superior officer who has had personal experience of the candidate should make the judgment as to fitness for promotion. The situation is much the same in the business and industrial world. Men who show progressively that they can take administrative responsibility are often advanced rapidly over associates with other talents.

UTILIZING EXPERIENCED ADMINISTRATORS

One with sufficient administrative knack and experience, howsoever acquired, can put it to use in many fields. Proven administrative talent and responsible experience in one particular field of activity make it possible for one to adjust quickly to administrative responsibility in a quite different field. Thus specialized industrial concerns sometimes select a top executive from among the executives of an entirely different business activity. Successful cabinet officers and heads of government agencies are regularly recruited from the college world as well as from business and industry. Military leaders have made good as college executives. A successful seminary rector with no other administrative experience has been known to make an outstanding university president.

In a word, one who has acquired administrative know-how in any one area of considerable responsibility can often adjust quickly to a new position, because he will have sufficient intelligence to want to learn as much as he can about his new field of operation before he begins to act with any assurance. There are, of course, exceptions. The dean of a college ought to be a logical choice for a presidency when there is a vacancy to be filled. This would especially be true if the dean was actually the number-two executive in the college and had firsthand familiarity with all the important business which passed through the president's office. But the logical choice is not invariably the best choice. A very knowledgeable and effective dean could be a poor president if he has a real distaste for a president's responsibilities or is disqualified by personality, by temperament, or for some other substantial reason. For similar reasons a good director of admissions could be completely out of place as an academic dean. Thus a favorable judgment as to an individual's probable fitness for a definite post will require more than testimony as to his previous administrative experience.

Use of temporary Administrators

When there is very little time for choice in filling a position which a member of the Religious Community ought to occupy, and the most likely prospect has only moderate experience but is young and willing and has the requisite ability, it is sometimes possible and advantageous to bring in an experienced administra-

tor on a temporary basis. The temporary appointee might either
be a retired administrator or one on loan.

A number of the larger institutions of higher education are
quite inexorable in enforcing a retirement rule. An administrator
in excellent health and at the peak of his efficiency is automatically retired on reaching the specified age, although he may have
several useful years ahead of him. One who has been released from
his college because he has reached the normal retirement age, is
often able and willing to fill an administrative post temporarily,
to give the advantage of his knowledge and experience to another
institution, and to have a part in the instruction of a younger educator who will eventually take his place. Suitable salary arrangements, combined with retirement income, are within the means of
a smaller institution, which otherwise could not possibly compete in the college world for the services of a man of comparable
experience. Men of this calibre upon retirement are being put to
good use in a number of colleges.

The writer knows of a distinguished law librarian who was retired from one of the large private universities and took over the
job of building up an excellent law library at a Catholic university.
After a few years, when his task was completed, he retired again,
only to answer the plea of another private university to help in
building up the law library there. An able woman educator, having retired as dean of a state college, took over as academic dean
at a new Catholic co-educational college conducted by a Religious
Community of men. It was her avowed purpose to build up a good
academic program and then pass on the deanship to a member of
the Religious Community. Many other examples could be cited.
But the point is that competent persons are available, if one
knows where to locate them. Better still, one must be able to get
a lead in knowing of an administrator's projected retirement, if he
is to be contacted before someone else has signed him up.

Another possibility for finding temporary assistance in such an
emergency as we have been discussing is to borrow the services
of an administrator from another college or university. This
would have to be arranged, of course, through personal contact
between the presidents of the lending and the borrowing institutions, and would involve a leave of absence for a definite

period of time. In such a situation the host institution would be expected, of course, to meet not only the full salary requirements of the lending institution, but also to take care of all extra expenses for transportation, moving, housing, and so on.

Although Catholic colleges rarely grant leaves to members of their administrative personnel, such leaves are frequently granted by non-Catholic institutions, both public and private—especially the larger institutions. Very often these leaves are granted at government request for services in various government capacities. But they are also granted for special projects under private auspices. Sometimes large institutions welcome the opportunity for an able assistant or associate dean to be placed temporarily in a situation where there will be more chance for him to exercise initiative and responsibility.

Religious Orders comprising more than one province often overlook a rich source of help, when they fail to borrow or exchange personnel between provinces. Within the same Order one would expect to find far more of this than actually takes place.

Competent Administrators Important

To keep in the race for survival today, a college must continue to make forward progress. Nothing will do more to slow up this progress or halt it altogether than sudden changes in administrative personnel and the appointment of Religious, who have had no previous experience, to responsible administrative posts. It may be that learning on the job is the best way to get this experience, but this learning should be made possible for the learner as understudy or assistant to an experienced administrator. To appoint a Religious to an important college administrative post, leaving everything to the virtue of obedience, seems an act of presumption on the part of the appointing officials. From a spiritual point of view it may not be unfair to the Religious, but from every point of view it is unfair to the college and its clientele.

CHAPTER 10

Faculty Organization

IT IS GENERALLY ACCEPTED in higher educational circles that teaching members of the faculty should participate in both policy-making and administration. Yet what has been accepted in theory does not always work out effectively in practice. The "small" college of today is larger than the small college of a decade ago—in enrollment, in faculty and in facilities—but it is not appreciably nearer to the university in either size or structure: it is somewhere in between. It is only reasonable to expect, therefore, that neither the general faculty meetings of former years nor the multidivisional system of the university will suit the college's need for faculty organization. The college must draw on both its own experience and the experience of the university in adapting and fashioning for itself practicable methods for faculty participation in policy-making and administration.

The college or university which numbers its faculty members in the hundreds and offers courses in many branches of learning must, for efficient operation, have schools, divisions, and departments with consequent multiplication of deans, directors and chairmen. It also has the problem of preserving some measure of unity, which these various operational units tend to challenge. The college of moderate size, with a full-time faculty of not more than a hundred or so, has no need for all the divisions and sub-divisions of the larger institution. But it does need some faculty organization, some analogous grouping arranged to suit its own needs and conditions.

OVER-ORGANIZATION

It would seem that many Catholic colleges of moderate size have taken much of their organizational structure from the larger institutions. In some instances there will be almost as many departments as there are subject-matter fields, each with its own chairman. Further complications result when a divisional arrangement, with additional chairmen, is superimposed on the departmental structure. The absurdity becomes immediately apparent if one compares the organizational structure of the faculty with the number of faculty members. Sometimes there will be almost as many chairmen of divisions, departments, and standing committees as there are full-time faculty members. This may present a faculty organization on paper but it cannot really function. Over-organization is partly, perhaps, a heritage from the days of small and predominantly Religious faculties, when no real organization was necessary. There was apt to be no more than one faculty member for each subject-matter field, who was both "department" and "head" of department because there was no one else in the same field. The faculty functioned as a body in policy-making and administration. Then titles and departments had neither the attraction nor the financial implications which are present today. When these educational trappings were adopted, it often happened that this was done without sufficient consideration of the logic, the necessity, or the long-term implications of either titles or departments.

A FUNCTIONAL ORGANIZATION

Every college should have a functional faculty organization to suit its needs and size. A college of moderate enrollment cannot afford to spread its faculty members over many departments and divisions. It can hardly expect to have both departments *and* divisions, with departments organized according to subject-matter fields and divisions grouping these departments according to common interests. If it is to have a functional faculty organization for both administrative and curricular purposes, the number of faculty units should be kept to a minimum. No fixed number can be arbitrarily prescribed, but it is possible to suggest a procedure whereby each college can decide for itself what shall be the number of functional faculty units and how they shall be composed. This can be accomplished by grouping together subject-matter fields, making allowances for community of interests and numerical balance.

A selected group of faculty members serving under a chairman can be considered a defensible unit, if the members are engaged in teaching in the same or in related subject-matter fields and can benefit from mutual collaboration, and if there are enough members in the group to make it possible to hold meetings, conduct discussions, and undertake certain delegated responsibilities. It is desirable to keep the various faculty units in numerical balance as far as possible, and to have as few of them as may be consistent with efficient operation. It is preferable that these faculty units be known as departments rather than divisions. By thus pre-empting the word "department" there will be less possibility of referring to each subject-matter field as a department in itself. While it may be difficult to compress departments in the beginning, it will be easier to expand and divide them as a college develops—a procedure which would be more difficult if they are originally "divisions."

ORGANIZING DEPARTMENTS

Each college must decide for itself the number of functional departments which it can justify, based upon an analysis of its own faculty and the local situation. Perhaps the simplest way to make this decision would be to list on separate index cards the various subject-matter fields in which courses are now offered, such as English, history, philosophy, and so forth. Next, list on each card the full-time teachers in the respective field and also the part-time teachers, with the proviso that a person may be listed on only one card. If a teacher handles courses in more than one subject-matter field, a decision must be made as to the field in which he or she is to be listed.

The numerical strength of a department must depend necessarily on the full-time members, and on such part-time teachers as are available for regular attendance at meetings. Faculty members with administrative duties, who are engaged full time on the campus but carry a light teaching schedule, can also be included. Instructors who are on campus only for stated periods each week can be omitted.

With the cards listing faculty members by subject-matter fields, it should be possible to see at a glance faculty strengths and weaknesses on a subject-matter basis. The chances are that out of eighteen or more subject-matter fields many will be found to lack the numerical strength for departmental status. It is also possible to see, with due regard for community of interests, what combinations will provide the numerical strength for functional units. Some combinations are clearly logical and can be made readily. Others have to be rationalized a bit. The number of departments may range between five and nine, depending on the local situation. A basic arrangement for six departments may be explained briefly as follows:

Theology and Philosophy. The grouping of these two disciplines in one department should contribute to better correlation in scheduling courses, so that students may get first those philosophy courses which will prepare for certain theology courses.

Fine Arts. No apology is necessary for grouping art, music, and drama in one functional department. A fine arts building providing joint facilities for these disciplines is now considered a "must" at most Catholic colleges for women.

Natural Science and Mathematics. Modern developments have broken down old barriers and emphasized the affinities of biology, chemistry, physics and mathematics. The college of moderate enrollment, which does not now have a separate science building with joint research facilities, either has it in the blueprint stage or regards it as an objective of its development program. The possibility of research grants for small colleges is considerably improved when joint projects are proposed.

Social Studies. Students frequently complain of overlapping and repetition of subject matter in these various courses. This department has an opportunity to make a real contribution in this area. Occasionally historians object to being grouped in the same department with economics, political science, geography and sociology. In such instances the designation "History and Social Studies" may be more readily accepted.

Language and Literature. English can be grouped with Latin, French, Spanish, German and other modern languages whenever it happens that the ancient and modern languages would not have sufficient members for a functioning department. There is, of course, a community of interests here, especially with the modern emphasis on linguistics. If the ancient and modern languages have enough members to stand as a department, usually there will also be enough members in English and, as a result, two departments may be preferred.

Service Arts.   Many colleges have grouped the subject-matter areas considered to be outside the liberal arts tradition into a department of "Community Services." Some colleges now prefer the designation "Service Arts," "Practical Arts" or "Applied Arts." The reason is that colleges are increasingly providing various non-academic services for their local communities, such as lectures, concerts, dramatic productions, workshops, adult education courses and the like. These are not offered for academic credit. There is danger, therefore, of confusing community services of this type with an academic Department of Community Services.

A department of "Service Arts" in one college may include education, home economics, library science, medical technology, nursing and secretarial studies—depending on the local situation. In such cases the specific problems in education and nursing would have to be recognized. A Director of Teacher Training could be appointed, to be charged with the supervision of observation and practice teaching and the relationships with the various schools involved. Likewise there would have to be a Director of Nursing to supervise the clinical instruction of the nursing candidates and the relationships with the various hospitals and agencies involved. When either education or nursing, or both, are grouped with other subject-matter areas, it may be more acceptable to use "Professional and Service Arts" as the name of the department.

In colleges where either education or nursing, or both, loom large because of student enrollment, there would be sufficient faculty members to warrant separate departments. This will be the case at many colleges. This would mean the addition of two more departments, together with English as a separate department, and these would bring the number of departments up to nine. In some colleges the number of departments has been reduced to five by combining the Fine Arts and Languages and Literature into a Department of Humanities. This is not advisable when the number of faculty members in such a department is considerably in excess of that in any other department.

No mention has thus far been made of psychology because the decision as to where this subject-matter field should go, will depend on how the subject is taught in a particular college. If it is taught mostly from a guidance or educational point of view, it can be grouped with education. If the emphasis is on rational psychology, it could be grouped with philosophy. And if the emphasis is on experimental psychology, the chances are that it would be more at home with the natural sciences or, possibly, the social sciences.

ADVANTAGES OF FEWER DEPARTMENTS

The grouping of two or more subject-matter fields in a single department does not subordinate any one field of learning to another, nor does it mean that one discipline shall dominate another. It does not denote a consolidation or merger of courses. It need have no effect on the majors or minors that are offered. It is not a matter of academic classification but simply of administrative organization. It will eliminate the one-, two-, and three-men departments and provide functional departments to which definite responsibilities can be assigned. It will be easier to find among the faculty from five to nine effective department chairmen rather than eighteen or twenty. It will be easier for the dean of the college to be in regular communication with five or nine chairmen rather than with two or three times that number. At the same time the functioning of these departments will help greatly to relieve the dean of an overburden of details. In some instances at least, it will assist the business office in both budget preparation and control.

Finally, this broader concept of membership in a department necessarily brings closer together members of various disciplines. It will facilitate and make possible that wider interdisciplinary understanding and collaboration which, although earnestly desired, is so difficult to attain in the larger colleges and universities.

Certain administrative responsibilities can be assigned to these functional departments. These responsibilities are delegated to each department through the chairman and could include such duties as the following: the holding of regular meetings at stated intervals; the initiation of revisions in curricula and course descriptions, for submission to the dean; the academic guidance of students in their major fields; promoting use of the library by faculty and students; submitting budget recommendations, and so on. The members must also assist the chairman in keeping up to date the department's file of course syllabi and other matters of record, and in taking such departmental assignments as may be given them from time to time.

Since the success of these faculty units must depend largely on the several chairmen, it is suggested that chairmen be appointed yearly by the president in consultation with the dean. The chief criterion for appointment should be ability to do the work, not seniority, rank, or academic degrees. Yearly appointments make it possible to ease out the chairman who does not function efficiently, to reappoint repeatedly when this is indicated, and to have rotation whenever this is practicable. Above all, it is important to keep the chairmanship of a department from becoming a super-rank to which a faculty member has a prescriptive claim.

General Faculty Meetings

It should not be assumed, because of the emphasis on functional faculty departments, that there is not an important place for general faculty meetings. At times there are matters of general policy that effect the entire faculty—for example, a change in the grading system—on which a consensus of the entire faculty is desirable. In a case like this the initial study and a definite recommendation should be the work of an *ad hoc* faculty committee. But the recommendation of this committee should ultimately be discussed before a general faculty meeting to see if there is a consensus for or against, or for a formal vote before final approval by the Administrative Council. But once the faculty has grown beyond the comfortable proportions of an intimate meeting, there is reason to doubt that there can be much direct participation in either policy-making or administration through these meetings.

General faculty meetings can also serve other purposes. They can be devoted to inspirational, informative, cultural and social purposes. They can serve as a forum for the president of the college to announce new plans or projects; for brief reports from college officials or faculty members who have recently attended important educational meetings of general interest; for a talk by a visiting educator or other appropriate speaker; for a panel discussion by selected faculty representatives on some debatable topic or book, to be followed by a general discussion; for a faculty committee report that is of general interest; and for other similar purposes.

The business to be presented at these meetings should be such as will tend to draw the faculty together, not something that will lead to wrangling or division. The length of these meetings should be carefully restricted so as not to tire or bore. This will also allow time for an informal social hour. At least one meeting a year could take the form of a dinner at which the wives and husbands of lay faculty members could be present. If wisely conceived and well planned, these meetings can serve to bring the faculty together as a whole and can do much to build up *esprit de corps*.

CHAPTER 11

The Lay Faculty

ALL CATHOLIC COLLEGES today have a "mixed" faculty, that is a faculty composed of laymen and laywomen as well as priests and Religious Brothers or Sisters. The total number of lay faculty members now exceeds the total number of priests and Religious by two to one, and the ratio is steadily increasing. In the larger institutions lay teachers greatly outnumber priests and Religious. There are still a few colleges where lay members of the faculty are very much in a minority. For the most part these are the smaller colleges, and usually conducted by Sisters.

In colleges operated by Religious Communities in the early days, lay members of the faculty were engaged as a matter of necessity, until properly qualified Religious could be prepared. But no one questions today that lay faculty members have a distinctive contribution to make to Catholic colleges and have come to stay. They would be included on the faculty of a college even though the Religious Community could fully staff the institution with its own members.

A UNIFIED FACULTY

It is important to a college that its Religious and lay faculty members be treated as one body, because the welfare of a college

94

depends in no small measure upon a close-knit faculty. The actual situation, however, differs from college to college, sometimes markedly. In some cases there is an admirable spirit of unity between Religious and lay personnel on the faculty. Laymen and laywomen have been brought in as collaborators with the Religious in the work of both administration and teaching. Excellent working relationships exist: there is mutual trust and confidence, and equal dedication to the ideals of the college and the work of education. In other instances there seems to be a distinct line of cleavage between lay and Religious. Such cleavage is harmful to the college. There is no valid reason why it should exist. If it is to be prevented, however, academic discrimination of any kind must be avoided, and Religious and lay faculty members must be dealt with similarly, especially in matters of rank, promotion, pay, department chairmanships, welfare provisions and the like.

There is no lack of good will on the part of Religious administrators of Catholic colleges in wanting lay faculty members to be an integral part of the college and to feel completely at home. But sometimes, through indirection, distinctions are made which contribute to divisiveness. At one college, for example, a *lay faculty council* was appointed by the president to look after the interests of lay members of the faculty. Although established with the very best of motives, such a council may tend to create the very divisiveness which it seeks to avoid. At least this was the opinion of some of the lay faculty members. A faculty welfare committee on which both Religious and lay faculty members serve would be quite a different matter. Such a committee might also help to develop in Religious faculty members a better understanding of the problems of their lay colleagues.

In another college a somewhat similar situation was in danger of arising by default. The administration had just approved the formation of a local chapter of AAUP to which it was expected that only lay members of the faculty would belong. Although it could be argued that membership in this organization would be of little if any advantage to Religious faculty members, their complete abstention from membership might be an obstacle to faculty integration. At least some members of the Religious faculty should belong to, and be active in, such a chapter if it is established at their college. This membership seems particularly important to those of us who see AAUP used more as a kind of trade union for the defense of its members than as a truly professional organization for the maintenance of professional standards.

Among the lay faculty members of Catholic colleges will be found a good proportion of non-Catholics. There is nothing new about this except in colleges which have only recently begun to employ lay faculty members. Thus one institution known to the author had, during a fifty-year period that began early in the first decade of this century, only two deans in one of its schools, both of them non-Catholics. Both deans had been appointed to their posts from the faculty and both of them died in office shortly before reaching retirement age.

The service of non-Catholic professors has in the past been generally satisfactory to Catholic colleges. At least the writer has never heard of complaints from administrators. It is assumed, of course, that non-Catholics are selected for their academic standing in teaching fields where there is not a distinctively Catholic point of view. It is also taken for granted that they be persons of good character whose lives are morally above reproach. But this latter requirement is fully as important in the case of the Catholic professor as it is with non-Catholic.

A mixture of Catholics and non-Catholics on the faculties of Catholic colleges seems to be a particularly advantageous arrangement today. In the friendly associations that should be encouraged between Catholic and non-Catholic colleges, these non-Catholic faculty members can be a distinct help. They can also contribute to good public relations in other ways. For example, their testimony to acquaintances outside the college that there is no denial of academic freedom and no religious prejudice at the college will carry conviction with those who might discount a similar statement from a Catholic. Students likewise have something to gain from this practical demonstration of the way in which all men of good will must be encouraged to work together for objectives which they hold in common.

Welfare Provisions

As long as lay members constituted a minority of the faculty
of a Catholic college, there never seemed to be any need for
published policies on promotion, rank and tenure. At least there
was never any pressure for such policies among lay faculty members. In colleges where it was a matter of settled policy to engage
lay faculty members, whenever it was apparent that there was
mutual satisfaction between college and lay faculty member it
was taken for granted that the association was an enduring one
as long as the lay member wished to continue, even though there
was never any mention of tenure. When the question of tenure
first began to be raised, there seemed to be little use for it in
Catholic colleges where the only members of the faculty who
seemed to lack "tenure" were the Religious members. They were,
and still are, subject to removal or transfer on short notice without
any question of "due process." This is one reason why Catholic
colleges have been relatively slow to adopt and publish definite
policies on these matters.

But conditions are quite different today. Lay faculty members
have a permanent place on the faculties of Catholic colleges and
universities, where on the average they now outnumber Religious
faculty members. Furthermore, they are a different breed of faculty members who often have family responsibilities, attach great
importance to "security," and want to see it set down in black and
white. They are concerned about initial terms of employment,
about promotion and rank and tenure, about the ever-burgeoning
list of fringe benefits which embrace both the present and the
future.

There are two extremes to be avoided in handling such matters
as appointments, rank, promotion, tenure and termination of
appointments. One extreme is to publish policies without thinking
them through in all their ramifications, the other is to have no
published policies but to endeavor to suit the policy to the particular situation.

Experience in visiting Catholic colleges inclines the writer to
believe that some colleges have published policies on appoint-

ments, rank, promotion, tenure and termination of appointments without having thought these policies through and without considering the implications for the particular college. It may be that these policies were taken over bodily from another college, because prospective faculty members ask about such things or because accrediting associations expect a college to have such policies. In any event, it did not seem that the published policies were the result of careful study.

The writer once visited a small woman's college conducted by a Religious Community of women. The college had recently published a handbook which, among other things, stated that a faculty member who had a one-year appointment would be notified by the first of February if his appointment was not to be renewed for the following academic year. Now it happened that the college had been prevailed upon to engage a refugee professor under a one-year agreement. Shortly after the beginning of the second term it became evident that the professor was not performing satisfactorily. Among other things his command of English was not all that had been represented. So the president of the college came to the conclusion that they could not engage the man for a second year. Accordingly, *blissfully unaware of the policy announced in the college's handbook,* the president informed the professor sometime after the first of February that the college would not be able to engage him for the following year. Whereupon the professor firmly informed the president that he would be in the employ of the college for the following year, and quoted the relevant statement from the faculty handbook. Although not a member of AAUP, he lost no time in writing to that organization, and the usual type of correspondence ensued. The moral is that if a college publishes a policy it ought to be prepared to abide by it, otherwise it would be better to have no policy at all.

The other extreme is to have no fixed policies on matters that affect the welfare of lay faculty members. It would seem that some Religious faculty members and administrators lack a sympathetic understanding of what a lay faculty member understands by security. They fail to see why he is highly conscious of those factors which enhance or threaten his feeling of security. The fact of the matter is that the Religious faculty member, as an individual, has no problem of economic security because the Religious Community is obligated to take care of him. As there is no assurance of "tenure" for the Religious faculty member, the whole idea of tenure may have little practical significance for him. Possibly there is a parallel in the situation of the rich young man who has no conception of the value of a dollar because he never had to earn a dollar by working for it.

DEFINITE POLICIES

Definite policies on such important items as salary, promotion, rank and tenure are of considerable importance to lay faculty members because they are vital to their feeling of security. It is important, therefore, for *all* Catholic colleges to have well-thought-out policies on these and other matters that affect the welfare of the lay members of their faculties. These matters merit careful study. There must be an evaluation of what is possible for the college to do in its present circumstances, and what it should aim to do in the immediate future. After these policies have been reduced to writing, the administration should inform the faculty of them; but it should not be in too much of a hurry to *publish* them—in a faculty handbook, for example—until they have received further consideration and even been given a period of trial.

In response to frequent requests that he suggest what he considers to be adequate policies, the writer will discuss these matters briefly in this chapter and then reduce them to corresponding policy statements which will be found in APPENDIX V.

Certainly every college ought to have a definite policy governing appointments to the faculty and a procedure for separation from the faculty. In between, there ought to be policies on rank, promotion and tenure. Of course, there must also be a salary policy; but on this we can make a few observations later so as not to confuse matters now. Anything like suggesting a salary scale will be avoided because this is likely to differ from area to area, from college to college, and from year to year. Policies on the other provisions will be more stable and more generally applicable.

APPOINTMENTS

Procedures for recruiting new faculty members will differ somewhat from college to college. In the smaller college the president may assume the full responsibility for all the details of recruiting, interviewing, and engaging new faculty members. Obviously he will consult with the dean and the appropriate department chairmen. In other institutions the dean or the department chairman may be principally responsible. But in most colleges the finding of new faculty members has become such a chore that many people must engage in the search.

The authority for the appointment and promotion of faculty members is vested legally in the board of trustees, on the nomination or recommendation of the president. Usually this power is largely delegated to the president and the results of his efforts are merely reported to the board. In any event, it is generally conceded that the president has the prime responsibility for building up the faculty of the college.

New members of the faculty are usually engaged on a probationary or temporary basis. This is known as a *term* appointment and may be for one or two years, subject to renewal. Part-time faculty members or lecturers are always considered term appointments. These appointments terminate at the close of the period agreed upon unless they are renewed by a specified date. If an appointment is not to be renewed, due notice of this should be given to the faculty member; but there is no *obligation* either on the college or on the appointee to renew a term appointment.

Faculty members may also be given permanent or continuous appointments. Such an appointment is usually granted only to the faculty member who has been engaged at the college for a certain period of years and who meets other specified conditions. In exceptional cases it may be granted immediately to an experienced faculty member who transfers from another college. A continuous appointment is subject to termination only on conditions that are mutually understood and accepted at the time of appointment.

Every appointment should be made by a formal agreement,

signed by the faculty member and by the president of the college or his authorized representative. Such an agreement should state the rank, salary, length of appointment, and all other important conditions of the relationship. Each prospective faculty member should receive a copy of the terms of appointment prior to his acceptance, so that his signature on the agreement will be evidence of his willingness to be bound by all its terms. No matter what policy on appointments a college may adopt, the most important point is that it should be prepared to carry out that policy faithfully. It must be recognized that, while a faculty agreement is in theory a bilateral contract, in practice the obligations it creates are largely one-sided, as no college is likely to sue a faculty member for breach of contract. But whether the agreement is enforceable or not, the average faculty member will honor the *moral* obligation it imposes on him. Even the failure of an individual to do so does not release the college from its own obligation. A sample policy statement covering appointments will be found on page 213.

TERMINATION OF APPOINTMENTS

Just as it is important to have a definite policy for appointing faculty members, so it is also important to have a definite procedure for the termination of faculty appointments before their normal date of expiration.

All faculty appointments, both term and continuous, can obviously be ended by mutual consent at any time before their termination date; but the faculty member can also terminate his appointment on his own volition by simply resigning. The termination policy of the college should attempt to set conditions for such a resignation, including a reasonable period of notice.

Faculty appointments are also terminated when the faculty member reaches the age of retirement officially established by the trustees of the college. The age specified varies from college to college; it may range between sixty-five and seventy, but it is seldom lower. The conditions governing retirement also vary. Sometimes retirement may be optional after a specified age and compulsory at a later age. When sixty-five is set as the retirement age, some colleges provide that a one-year, or a one-term, or a part-time appointment may be granted in individual cases at the discretion of the president and the board of trustees.

There is, no doubt, something arbitrary about compulsory retirement. Nevertheless, in the long run it is in the best interests of all concerned—teacher, student, and college. Without an automatic or compulsory retirement, each case has to be decided on an individual basis. In some cases this inevitably involves protest, heartache, and often bitterness.

The policy on age for retirement should apply to *all* faculty members, Religious as well as lay. Once rules have been established, it is easier to deal with the Religious faculty member who has grown old in the service of the college. Unable to recognize that he or she has passed the age of effective classroom teaching, such a person may be deeply hurt if singled out for compulsory retirement rather than prepared for it by knowledge of a set policy.

It must be said emphatically, however, that no college should have a "retirement for age" requirement unless it also has a funded retirement program for lay faculty members in addition to Federal Social Security (OASI) coverage. Probably the best known and most widely used plan is that provided by Teachers Insurance and Annuity Association. This non-profit agency was founded especially to assist colleges and universities in providing funded retirement programs for faculty members. The association also offers group insurance programs, notably in the field of "major medical" expense coverage.[1]

A policy statement on the termination of faculty appointments would be incomplete without establishing a procedure whereby the college may terminate *for cause* either a continuous appointment or a term appointment before its expiration date. Causes for termination are: conviction in the courts for a serious crime, grave moral delinquency, professional incompetence, physical or mental incapacity, and flagrant defiance of the ideals of the college.

It should be clearly recognized that the burden of proof in

---

[1] Greenough, William C. and King, Francis P., *Retirement and Insurance Plans in American Colleges* (New York: Columbia Univ. Press, 1959), 480 pages.

dismissing a faculty member for cause rests on the college administration. Before preferring charges or taking any other action the
college must have all the evidence in hand, review the relevant
agreement and related policy statements, and seek legal counsel.
When charges are preferred, the faculty member should have
every reasonable opportunity to contest the charges and to produce witnesses.

These cases can often be complicated and embarrassing, especially when moral delinquency is involved and the matter becomes public. Nevertheless, to protect the rights of the accused,
there must be no abridgment of due process; to this end, competent legal advice should be sought from the beginning. Furthermore, any slip-up in what is considered "academic" due process
will inevitably bring down on the college the wrath of certain
organizations which believe they have a mission to protect the
rights of the individual. In these matters it is well to have established procedures on the books, although it is to be hoped that a
college will rarely, if ever, have to invoke such procedures. A
sample policy statement on Termination of Appointments will be
found on pages 214 and 215.

TENURE

Tenure means the assurance of continuous appointment until
retirement age has been reached. It can be terminated only for
cause under conditions mutually understood and accepted at the
time of appointment. Causes which arise on the part of the appointee have already been mentioned. Other causes for termination by the college besides misconduct or grossly unsatisfactory
performance would be financial stringency, serious decrease in
enrollment, etc., which should always be demonstrable and in
good faith.

From the standpoint of the faculty member, tenure appears as
a necessary measure of security and a safeguard of academic freedom. Tenure may protect the uncooperative, the indifferent, even
the incompetent teacher once he has safely passed the hurdle of
probation, but this is a risk that has to be run in order to assure
the public of academic integrity. From the college point of view

tenure should be designed to give a tangible sense of security to those faculty members whom the college wishes to retain and would be very loath to lose.

In order to serve the best interests of the college, then, tenure should not be granted until there has been sufficient experience with a faculty member to be reasonably sure he or she will be a continuing asset to the college. At the same time a tenure policy should not be so rigidly tied to rank that adjustments cannot be made when this appears to be in the interest of the college. A sample tenure policy is given on page 215.

ACADEMIC FREEDOM

The writer has never experienced any particular difficulty with academic freedom in Catholic colleges. These colleges recognize that the desire for freedom is innate in man because the Creator endowed him with freedom of the will, which exempts him from any absolute necessity in choice or in action. But this priceless gift brings with it the responsibility to see that neither the rights of God nor of other men are infringed. Since man is not an isolated being, there is at least a moral necessity to limit his freedom. Academic freedom is only one segment of the freedom which free men possess. In common with all other kinds of freedom it cannot be absolute.

Consequently a Catholic college has no difficulty in recognizing the importance of protecting the freedom of the teacher in teaching and the freedom of the student in learning. It does expect, however, that a teacher in freely discussing his subject will "be careful not to introduce into his teaching controversial matter which has no relation to his subject." [2] Neither does a college question that a faculty member gives up no rights as a citizen, and that when he speaks or writes as a citizen he should be free from institutional prescription. It does expect, however, that when a faculty

---

[2] The quotations in this paragraph and the following one are from the official policy statement on "Academic Freedom and Tenure" of the ASSOCIATION OF AMERICAN COLLEGES which was adopted in January, 1941. This statement together with a later one on "Procedural Standards in Faculty Dismissal Proceedings" adopted in January, 1958, are reprinted for handy reference as APPENDIX VII of this book.

member speaks or writes as a citizen he will remember that "the public may judge his profession and his institution by his utterance. Hence he should at all times be accurate, should exercise appropriate restraint, [and] should show respect for the opinions of others." Again, when he is dealing with controversial matters, he is expected to make it clear that he speaks or writes "not as an institutional spokesman" but only in his capacity as a private citizen.

It is generally recognized that a church-related college, because of its religious objectives, may require certain limitations on freedom that might not apply to a different kind of institution —for example, a state university. Ordinarily we would take it for granted that one who freely accepts appointment to the staff of a Catholic college will have the prudence and courtesy not to attack or go contrary to the ideals for which the college stands. Experienced educators advise, however, that "limitations of academic freedom because of religious and other aims of the institution should be clearly stated in writing at the time of appointment."

It would seem to be prudent, therefore, that a Catholic college should include in its teaching agreement and faculty handbook some such brief statement as the following:

> Members of the faculty enjoy full academic freedom but they are not free, of course, to advocate and disseminate doctrines that are subversive of American political freedom and government or of the aims and purposes of this College, a Catholic institution, committed to the upholding of Christian faith and morality.

Faculty Rank and Promotion

With the increase in numbers of the lay faculty, the recognition of rank among faculty members and some system for advancement in rank are now incumbent upon a Catholic college as they are on any other college. In preparing such a policy it is hoped that the college has made two preliminary decisions. First, it has reduced the number of its academic departments to a workable minimum, consistent with the size of the college and its faculty, and has done away with the catalogue fiction of one-man or two- and three-men departments. Second, it has made an estimate of the number of professors and associate professors a college of its size and resources can afford to have, realizing that salary is closely tied to rank as well as to length of service and taking account of current salary scales. At least the college must recognize that there will have to be some over-all limitation on the number of faculty members in the higher ranks, based either on the number of academic departments or on a certain percentage of the full-time faculty.

Large institutions strive to keep a balance in faculty ranks by arbitrarily fixing a time limit on the employment of faculty members in the lower ranks. Thus an instructor is automatically separated from the university faculty, despite excellent qualifications and satisfactory service, if after a specified number of years of service he cannot be advanced to an assistant professorship because there are no vacancies. This policy does not seem to be either practicable or necessary for the average college. Sometimes good teachers are concerned more with the congeniality of their work at a small college than with rank. They may be willing to stay on permanently, even without definite assurance of advancement in rank, provided improvement in salary and tenure are not thereby jeopardized. For that reason, in the average small Catholic college, neither salary scale nor tenure ought to be too closely tied with rank.

In determining ranks, colleges customarily make a clear-cut distinction between full-time and part-time faculty members. Only full-time faculty members are considered eligible for rank. Part-time faculty members are not ranked but are frequently accorded the title of "lecturer" or "part-time instructor." In ascending order, the ranks usually granted to full-time faculty members are: instructor, assistant professor, associate professor, and professor. Some colleges do not have the rank of associate professor.

It is certainly desirable that a college should have an established set of minimum requirements for each rank. In ordinary circumstances these minimum requirements should be strictly observed, but there may be occasions when exceptions ought to be made. Unusual circumstances may arise when an exception seems to be in the best interests of the college. The established requirements should *not* be considered so inflexible that the president and board of trustees would hesitate to make any exceptions.

For example, an exceptionally able teacher with less than the specified number of years of experience might be promoted or brought into the faculty at a higher level than that indicated by the minimum requirements. Again, there might be good reasons why a teacher transferring from another institution should be initially appointed to an associate or full professorship, even with tenure, although lacking any previous experience at the college to which he is being appointed.

There are also occasions when specified degree requirements may be waived because of unusual qualifications of a different kind, or because of variant types of professional training and experience, as happens, for example, in the fine arts. None of these exceptions gainsay the importance of having established minimum requirements for rank as the normal guide lines for advancement.

In considering the promotion of a faculty member to a higher rank there are, of course, other qualifications besides academic background and ability in his field which ought to be evaluated, particularly in a small college in which teamwork is necessary: loyalty to the college as judged by the person's willingness to serve beyond the call of duty; devotion to the declared ideals of the college as evinced by a willingness to abide by these ideals and to promote them, as far as possible, in students; interest in students as evinced by willingness to give outside assistance where necessary, and to confer and counsel with them as may be required; willingness to cooperate with administration and faculty by faithfully serving on committees, attending faculty meetings, and sharing such administrative tasks as may be assigned from time to time.

In publishing a statement of requirements for promotion, it is important to make it clear that advancement to a higher rank does not necessarily follow when one has fulfilled the requirements prescribed for that particular rank. In other words, advancement to higher rank is not automatic. Three other conditions must be verified: there must be an opening in the rank to which advancement is sought; there must be a recommendation through the proper channels, testifying that the candidate for advancement has met the established norms; finally, there should be such approval by the president or board of trustees as may be required by the bylaws of the college.

It is usually preferable that requests or recommendations for promotion originate with the department chairman in written form, and be channeled through a faculty committee on promotion—if there is one—to the dean and the president. Final approval will rest with the president, if he has been delegated this authority by the board of trustees; otherwise, it will depend on the board itself.

Definite published policies on rank and promotion, as well as those previously mentioned, contribute to the peace of mind of faculty members. From the administrative point of view they contribute to stability and orderly procedure. They guard against misunderstanding and conflict. But whatever policies may be adopted, it goes without saying that these policies, particularly on rank and promotion, must apply equally to both Religious and lay members of the faculty. A sample statement of policy on "rank and promotion" will be found on pages 215-217.

FINANCIAL COMPENSATION

The financial compensation which lay faculty members receive, is not limited to actual compensation in cash. It includes whatever may have been withheld from the salary as payments for social security, annuity, insurance and the like, as well as what the college pays for these and other faculty benefits. All of these items must be considered in calculating the total compensation paid to faculty members. Too often faculty members themselves think only in terms of what they actually receive in cash. But the college must take account of the entire salary and the cost of any "fringe benefits" in planning a faculty salary scale.

There is no intention to discuss salary scales or fringe benefits[3] here. That would take us too far afield, and whatever we might write would very likely be outmoded in the near future. But a few general observations may be helpful, especially to colleges

---

[3] See Ingraham, Mark H., *The Outer Fringe: Faculty Benefits Other Than Annuities and Insurance* (Madison, Wisc.: University of Wisconsin Press, 1965), 304 pages.

which are only now beginning to feel the pressure for published salary scales (with greatly increased salaries and yearly increments) and for the adoption of various fringe benefits. If these colleges have never had to worry in the past about large and ever-growing salary budgets, for the simple reason that they have had very few lay faculty members, there is danger that they will overdo things.

The writer has seen faculty salary scales in small Catholic women's colleges that would do credit to a large university. These colleges seem to think they can afford such generous salary scales, because the lay faculty is only now beginning to grow and no salaries will actually be paid in the higher brackets for several years to come. A few years hence, will these colleges be able to meet the payroll? That is a question which ought to be figured out ahead of time.

These colleges would arrive at a more realistic salary scale if they would make the attempt to project their salaries over a ten-year period, taking into consideration advancement in rank, salary increments, number of additional lay teachers required to take care of increased enrollment, as well as all other rising costs in operating the college. Such a study might also help to influence the Religious Community to embark on a more intensive program of graduate study, in order to prepare a larger number of Religious as college teachers. An increase in contributed services would be a very practical way of trying to offset the salary budget for a mounting lay faculty.

Some Catholic colleges have committed themselves to sizable yearly and across-the-board salary increments. This is commendable as a temporary measure where faculty salaries have been abnormally low. But as a fixed pattern it could quickly get out of hand and be very harmful to the morale of the faculty. Once salaries have reached a respectable level, it would seem that future salary increases should be wholly on a merit basis, or at least partly, so as not to eliminate the incentive motive.

In the face of all the pressures for faculty welfare provisions that are now being brought to bear on college administrations, no college should be stampeded into action until it has made proper studies; nor should it blindly adopt the policies of other colleges.

Whatever a college does by way of welfare provisions ought to be fiscally sound. Since it is not likely that every college will be able to adopt all the requested faculty benefits, certain priorities ought to be established. The number-one priority, of course, is an adequate salary scale, as generous as the college can afford. Following closely behind, there should be a retirement annuity program and some group insurance provisions. Whatever else a college can or may want to do will depend on its resources and various circumstances. In this area the writer believes in being conservative.

CHAPTER 12

A Faculty Handbook

A FACULTY HANDBOOK can be a useful administrative tool if it serves as a ready source of information on college matters which have, or should have, frequent reference value for faculty members. It should be a compendium of college procedures and practices which are of immediate concern to all faculty members, a *vade mecum* for the new instructor as well as a handy reminder for the seasoned veteran.

Most colleges have faculty handbooks. But of all their publications, this one often seems to show evidence of the least care and imagination. It is seldom up to date. One might easily get the impression that these handbooks are a necessary nuisance, which one must have on hand for the use of members of an evaluation team when a college is in line for accreditation or re-accreditation.

Suggestions for a Handbook

It is not possible, of course, to draw up a blueprint of the ideal faculty handbook. But one who has had occasion to examine many handbooks critically may have acquired impressions and opinions that are worth sharing. The following observations are made on the assumption that a faculty handbook is intended for the faculty and that there is no reason for it to double as an administrative manual or as a depository for bylaws, either for the board of

111

trustees or for the administration. If it is intended for the faculty, it should contain only those items that may be presumed to have *frequent* reference value for faculty members.

Many handbooks are written in bylaw form. This makes for very uninteresting reading because of the format used for bylaws and because much bylaw material has very little direct reference to faculty members. This does not contribute to the use or value of a faculty handbook. College bylaws, whether for the board of trustees or for the administration of the college, should serve as a basic source of information in compiling the handbook, but it need not reproduce them. Thus the bylaws of the governing board should be the authority for the following brief statement which is all that need be said about the governing board in a faculty handbook.

The Board of Trustees

The Board of Trustees, comprising seven members, bears full and complete responsibility for the College as a corporate entity. It formulates and determines such general policies as may be deemed necessary for the administration and development of the College.

The bylaws for the administration of a college have greater reference value for faculty members and will be more useful in compiling the handbook. But the information contained therein ought for the most part to be selected and presented in brief and paraphrased form, not simply quoted from the bylaws. For example, a sentence or two should be sufficient to describe administrative officers whose duties are obvious or with whom faculty members have few direct relationships. Little need be said, for example, about the president and possibly about the dean, whose responsibilities are also fairly obvious unless he is handling tasks usually performed by a registrar or other college official. Thus:

The President

The President is the chief executive of the College and is ultimately responsible for all its activities.

The Academic Dean

The Academic Dean, the chief academic officer of the College, is directly responsible to the President for all academic activities, acts as his chief adviser, and discharges his duties during his absence.

It may be that more ought to be said about the dean, depending on the local situation. More ought also to be said, perhaps, about administrative officers, such as the registrar, the dean of students, the business manager, and the director of development, who have direct contacts with faculty members and must look to them for cooperation in getting their jobs done. Again this means a selective mention of the officer's duties with special reference to faculty members. The item on the registrar, for example, might read as follows:

The Registrar

The Registrar fulfills a number of duties which are of direct concern to faculty members. She has charge of all arrangements for registration and during that period will have to call for special assistance from faculty members.

She is responsible for the scheduling of classes, the assignment of classrooms, student class schedules, examination schedules, the sectioning of classes, where required, and the preparation of class lists.

Together with the Dean, she plans teacher schedules. Taken all together, this is a complex and laborious operation which deserves the understanding and cooperation of all faculty members. Only in exceptional circumstances should a faculty member request changes in class periods, classrooms, or teaching schedules.

The Registrar has the responsibility of receiving and recording all student grades, compiling class averages and ranks, and getting out the grade reports promptly to parents and other interested persons. In order to avoid unwarranted delay, faculty members are expected to turn in grades promptly and to observe the time limit announced by the Registrar.

She has the duty of collecting material for changes and revisions in the College catalogue and must have the cooperation of faculty members, particularly department heads, if she is to meet the printer's deadline.

Somewhat similar treatment may be required for the dean of students, the business manager, the director of development, and possibly other officials. But a sentence or two will ordinarily be sufficient for the director of admissions, the chaplain, and other officers.

Chart of Organization. The administrative setup can be further clarified by including a well-drawn Chart of Administrative Organization, which has been worked out carefully to match the Bylaws of Administration.

Faculty Organization. There should be complete information about faculty organization—about the departments and the responsibilities of department chairmen. There should also be complete information about standing faculty committees, their membership and duties. Also there should be full information about general faculty meetings. Here there can be no objection to taking this information over bodily from the Bylaws of Administration if it is presented there clearly and in detail.

Needless Repetition. The handbook should avoid needless repetition of material that is already available in sources readily accessible to faculty members. This does not mean that such items are not to be mentioned. It may be quite important to mention them briefly and then refer to an available source for further information. The following examples are given merely for their form and suggestive value:

Annuity Program

The College participates in the TIAA Program. Faculty members not already participants are included in this program after two years of teaching at the College. Contributions toward the building up of this funded retirement benefit are paid on a matching basis, half by the college and half by the faculty member. *For further information request TIAA folder from the Business Office.*

There are two reasons for not going into detail about the annuity program in the handbook. In the first place it has reference value only for the new faculty member who has not as yet been included. In the second place the information is already available in convenient form for those who require it. More detailed information may be required on other "fringe benefits" which would not otherwise be available in a convenient separate statement. Two additional examples of brief cross references follow:

Student Decorum

All members of the faculty are asked to require that the norms of conduct and good manners expected of............College students be observed at all times. Faculty members should be familiar with the regulations to be found in the Student's Handbook. If for any reason you have mislaid your copy, another may be obtained at the office of the Dean of Students.

Aims and Objectives

A statement of the general aims and objectives of the College will be found on page nine of the current catalogue. This statement, officially adopted by the Board of Trustees, was prepared by administration and faculty. All activities of the College, academic, departmental, religious, social, recreational and the rest, ought to be in harmony with these objectives.

The Format.   Whether a handbook should be printed, multi-lithed, or mimeographed is largely a matter of budget. But only while it is still in the tentative or trial stage should it be the product of a spirit duplicator. Above all else it should be readable. Individual items should be reasonably brief and attractively presented. This means that there should not be too much on a page. Headings and sub-headings should be used freely and with generous spacing to avoid crowding items together.

Details of Content.   A few principles to guide in the preparation of a faculty handbook have been enunciated and illustrated. Further details may be unnecessary, but the following suggestions for the contents of a faculty handbook have been drawn from a study of the handbooks of fifty Catholic colleges. Since a usable handbook requires an adequate table of contents and a good index, the suggested topics are so arranged as to provide the basic material for a table of contents comprised of only the words given in capital letters. The use of all of the topics, both those in capital letters and those in lower case letters, will give at least a basic index.

Suggested Topics

FOREWORD or INTRODUCTION

TABLE OF CONTENTS

THE ADMINISTRATION and CHART OF ORGANIZATION

CONTRACTUAL RELATIONS and STATUS OF FACULTY MEM-
BERS: appointments; outside employment; promotion; rank; retirement; salaries; teaching contract; tenure; termination of appointment.

PROFESSIONAL RESPONSIBILITIES OF FACULTY MEMBERS:
academic guidance of students; academic freedom; attendance at
meetings and conventions; faculty personnel files; membership in
learned societies; professional activities report; publication and research.

FACULTY ORGANIZATION: chairmen of departments; departments;
faculty committees; faculty meetings.

FACULTY BENEFITS: admission to athletic events; admission to
concerts and dramatic productions; admission to student social affairs; free tuition for family; insurance; leave of absence; retirement
benefits; sabbatical leaves; sick leaves; social security.

FACILITIES AND SERVICES AVAILABLE TO FACULTY MEM-
BERS: audio-visual aids; bulletin boards; duplicating services; educational supplies; lounge facilities; lunch facilities; mail service;
office space; parking; recreational facilities; secretarial services;
smoking areas; student assistants; telephones.

ADMINISTRATIVE REGULATIONS: academic dress; attendance
at college functions; college standards; course syllabi; dishonesty in
exams; faculty absence; faculty public relations; field trips; fire drills;
grades and grade reports; guest lecturers; recommendations for stu-

dents; schedule changes; scheduling college events; student absences; textbook changes; travel allowances; tutoring students.

INSTRUCTIONAL PROCEDURES: assignment of rooms; class periods; class policies and procedures; examinations; examination files; grading system; proctoring exams; special exams; teaching loads; teaching schedules; time schedules.

LIBRARY SERVICES: book requests or suggestions; faculty loan privileges; inter-library loans; reading lists; reserve books.

EXTRACURRICULAR DUTIES OF FACULTY MEMBERS: chaperonage; club moderators; public relations.

FACULTY RELATIONS WITH STUDENTS: academic counseling; admission to class; classroom management; office hours; student decorum.

RELATIONS WITH BUSINESS OFFICE AND BOOKSTORE: book orders; bookstore, budget; class record books; desk copies of textbooks; equipment; keys; maintenance and service needs; requisitions.

CAMPUS DIRECTORY

INDEX

The approximately one hundred topics listed above are all important enough to be included in a handbook, but the list is by no means exhaustive.

A Useful Addition. Some colleges have included in their handbooks a sort of who-to-see and where-to-go directory. This is designed to answer questions of the type: Where can I get this information? Where can I seek this authorization? Where do I report this? Information like the following could be helpful for such a section: Where does one reserve facilities for meetings? Where does one make arrangements for transferring, changing, missing a class? Where does one get classroom supplies, chalk, erasers, rollbooks? Where does one get audio-visual equipment?

Frequency of Publication. A faculty handbook should be kept reasonably up to date. Otherwise it is worse than useless. It should, therefore, be published as frequently as may be required to keep it current. This does not necessarily mean yearly publication. The faculty handbook envisaged here should ordinarily not have to be published more than once every two or three years. This presupposes that constantly changing information, like addresses and telephone numbers, is not included. One college provides for minor changes by leaving two or three vacant pages at the end of the handbook, which are marked as available for making notes and pasting in changes and revisions.

Date of Publication: In every edition of the handbook it should be possible to find the latest date of publication or revision. This can appear inconspicuously, preferably at the beginning or even at the end. The important thing is that every issue of the handbook be dated.

Handy Yearly Supplement. Early each September, one college president distributes to the faculty a supplement of several pages which can be slipped into the rear of the handbook. This supplement gives a complete directory of administrative officers and faculty members, with campus address and telephone, and the home address and telephone, of each one. There is also a complete list of the chairmen of academic departments, the chairmen and members of all standing committees, the directors and coaches of all student organizations, and the moderators of all student activities. Finally there is a list of the secretaries in the administrative offices. This is an excellent way to keep the faculty handbook up to date without putting out an edition every year or two.

CHAPTER 13

Managing Material Resources

IT IS GENERALLY RECOGNIZED that the conservation and management of the material resources of a college and the maintenance of its physical plant and facilities now constitute a separate area of college administration. It is customary for this area of administration to be headed by a single, top-echelon administrator, no matter what his title may be, who is directly responsible to the president of the college.

In this area of administration are handled the ordinary collection of revenue, the control of expenditures authorized in the budget, the purchasing of all supplies and materials, the payment of all invoices and other legitimate financial obligations, the bookkeeping and accounting, the service and maintenance of buildings and grounds, the management of the auxiliary enterprises of the college, such as dormitories, food services, bookstores and the like, and finally the personnel responsibility for welfare of all non-academic personnel of the college. Depending on the size of the college, these activities are distributed among various staff officers who report to the administrator who heads this area.

BUSINESS MANAGEMENT

The rapid growth of colleges in recent years, with the consequent increase in plant and in maintenance and operational costs, has made necessary many reforms in the business and financial organization of colleges. The days when individual teachers or departments could do their own purchasing are at an end. Slipshod methods in ordering equipment or supplies, or in paying bills, are gone. Instead we have centralized purchasing, competitive bidding, contract purchasing in bulk during favorable market periods, and warehousing if necessary. Bills are paid promptly to take advantage of time discounts, and many other ways of stretching the value of the dollar are now commonplace. Undoubtedly all this has interfered somewhat with the freedom and independence of the individual faculty member. There may even be a certain amount of regimentation. But no one advocates returning to the "good old days." Good business management is taken for granted.

Most colleges find it necessary to have professional business management with a competent full time staff and modern business machines and equipment. Otherwise, effective budgets and budgetary controls would not be possible, and inefficiency and waste would either bankrupt colleges or greatly deplete the funds available for strictly educational purposes. Certainly no Catholic college can afford to lag behind in the adoption of efficient and up-to-date business procedures.

THE BUDGET

A "college budget" may have different meanings for different people on the campus. It may point up financial problems to the president, but to the business officer it may mean chiefly figures that must be kept in balance. To the dean it may indicate that postponement of plans for new courses is inevitable, while to a department head it may mean heavier teaching assignments or a delay in plans for new equipment. To some faculty members it may signify merely another kind of administrative double talk. But, regardless of the point of view, the budget is an important and indispensable instrument for the efficient management of the financial resources of the college.

The budget is a detailed plan for the financial operation of the

college over a twelve-month period of time known as the fiscal
year. It is usually prepared several months in advance of the
beginning of the fiscal year. It is based on careful estimates of
anticipated income, of the expenditures required to cover the fixed
charges for operation, and of such other expenses as are judged
necessary or desirable. Since the average college never has enough
money to meet all its needs, there must be some order of priority
among expenditures permitted by the available funds.

The chief purpose of a budget is to keep expenditures within
income and to make it possible to spend money wisely and well.
For this reason it is essential that there be adequate control, at
least of the total budget. This implies in turn that there be an
efficient business office with an adequate accounting system and
an effective method for control. It is unthinkable that any college
would attempt to operate today without a yearly budget carefully
prepared and strictly followed.

It would take us too far afield to go into the mechanics of con-
structing a college budget. Fortunately there is plenty of literature available on this subject. In particular, *College and University Business Administration, Volume 1*,[1] gives essential information on budgets and a generous bibliography (page 173). It is sufficient to say here that if a college has the streamlined, functional
departments described previously in chapter 9 of this book, academic budgets should, as far as possible, originate with these
departments; and each department should be given a written
statement of its detailed budget at the time it is adopted by the
board of trustees.

In a college situation it is desirable that the general methods of
control permit reasonable flexibility on the departmental level, so
that the most economical requisitioning of supplies, equipment,
and other purchases may be possible within the funds available.
It is important also that there be incentives for the assumption of
responsibility at the departmental level. Thus it is not desirable to
have a procedure for the recapture of funds unused for a specific
budget item, because this tends to eliminate the incentive to adopt

---

[1] Published by AMERICAN COUNCIL ON EDUCATION, Washington 6,
D.C., 1952. A revised edition is expected in 1966.

a less expensive but adequate alternative. When the budget funds available in the department cannot be shifted to a more pressing or appropriate use, there is no reward for being frugal.

Some Religious Communities seem to have difficulty in adjusting their internal policies, methods, and customs to the requirements of conducting a modern college. Nowhere is this more evident than in their fiscal policies, which are more in harmony with the practices of a generation ago and are far removed from the policies, methods and controls now necessary in college administration. Many unnecessary hardships for Religious personnel in college administration are created by this gap.

No one questions the fact that a Religious Community must exercise certain fiscal controls, just as the college administration must exercise certain fiscal controls. But a carefully prepared college budget ought to serve the purposes of both controls. If it is prepared well in advance of the fiscal year, it may be processed for authoritative approval through both religious and civil channels in ample time. The religious approval required by the constitutions of the Religious Community comes from the "house chapter" or its equivalent, and then from the major religious superior and his or her council. The legal approval required by state law comes from the board of trustees.

Once the budget has received the approval of the board of trustees of the college, no further recourse to this body is required by law for the expenditure of funds authorized in the budget. Only when there must be substantial changes in the budget, or expenditure of funds not contemplated in the budget, is it necessary to have further recourse to the board of trustees.

The author knows of no reason why a similar procedure should not be followed in regard to religious approval, which is also concerned more with "extraordinary expenditures" than with current expenses. When contemplated extraordinary expenditures are included in the annual budget, as is proper, and the entire budget receives religious approval, further recourse to house chapters or religious superiors should not be necessary—except where substantial changes in the budget or the expenditure of substantial funds, not originally contemplated therein, are required. The situation should be the same as with the board of trustees. Any other procedure greatly handicaps the college with unwarranted delays and increases the already considerable complexities in the financial operation of a college.

It is surely an anachronism to require a Religious member of an academic department, in addition to fulfilling the purchasing requirements of the college, to get the approval of a local religious superior for every single expenditure made under a departmental budget which has already received religious approval as part of the whole college budget. No lay member of a department has to submit to this additional red tape. This situation, which the author has occasionally encountered, indicates that the personal expenditures of the Religious are being confused with what is in reality a departmental expenditure of the college. In the first instance there is a direct relationship with the obligation of the vow of poverty which does not apply at all to the second instance.

LAY BUSINESS MANAGER

Many Catholic colleges operated by priests or Brothers have discovered the advantages of lay business-management. No matter how competent and knowledgeable in business affairs a priest, Brother, or Sister may be, business and commercial people will seldom give them credit for this. As a consequence there is a tendency on the part of some representatives of business concerns to "cut corners" in their dealings with the college, or to play on the sympathy or religious sensibilities of the Religious business officer. A priest or Religious does not wish to seem distrustful of such people, to haggle with them, or to appear hardbitten. It is here that the layman as business manager has the advantage. In the first place he is more likely to be dealt with on a strictly businesslike basis as one who knows his way around in the business world. Even if he is not given this recognition, he will have no hesitation in quickly calling a halt to any attempt to take advantage of the college.

Of late years an increasing number of Catholic women's colleges have come to see the value of a competent layman as controller or "watchdog" over the business activities of the college.

This has been found particularly effective in dealing with past-due accounts and in collecting old accounts. A layman's activities in these matters does not stir up the resentment that sometimes falls to the lot of the priest or Religious. There is seldom any attempt to play on the "religious charity" of the layman, nor does he have to listen to the irrelevant argument that more consideration is due to the petitioner because of his fidelity in contributing to his parish church. A layman is also more effective in dealing with non-academic lay personnel, with businessmen and contractors, especially in arranging for the estimates and competitive bidding that are involved in central purchasing and in the maintenance of buildings and grounds.

The ideal arrangement in a college conducted by a Religious Community is to have both a Religious and a layman in the business office, who will work closely together and complement each other. The Religious can be called the procurator or the treasurer. The title does not matter so long as the Religious has business and financial know-how, or the ability to acquire it, and the willingness to make the best cooperative use of the talents of the lay business manager.

The chief difficulty is, of course, to find the right layman for business manager. One must be reasonably sure in advance of the qualifications of the man to be engaged. A college which is served by a large auditing firm with offices in many cities usually has no great difficulty in finding the right man through this firm.

Colleges which have had the good fortune to employ competent business managers have found that the greater efficiency and economy often more than compensate for the salaries that are paid out. Moreover the good business setup we envisage is an excellent place for young Religious to serve an apprenticeship for future assignments in other institutions conducted by the Religious Community.

LONG-RANGE FINANCIAL PLANNING

Attention has been directed in recent years to the importance of long-range planning for privately supported colleges and universities.[2] Central to such planning is the five-to-ten-year budget. This is an attempt on the part of the college, based on certain carefully reasoned assumptions, to project its annual budget ahead for a period of five to ten years. The thought and reflection required to draft a long-range budget provide in many ways a very salutary and sobering experience for a college administration.

In the first place, it requires that at least a tentative enrollment goal be set for a five-to-ten-year period, with estimated yearly increments. Against these enrollment estimates must be matched the teaching staff, the buildings, and the facilities required. The resulting operating and capital expenditures must then be calculated. Finally, it must be determined how, and from what sources, the necessary funds are to be obtained. How high shall student tuition and fees be raised? How much money must be raised by capital fund drives and when? How much money is to be obtained through gifts, grants, etc.? The resulting calculations may show that it will be more economical to lower the sights on enrollment or, possibly, to raise the enrollment goal.

Such a long-range budget must be subject, of course, to yearly re-examination and revision in the light of experience with the current year's budget. It may also happen that clearer forecasts for the future become possible. Once this long-range budget has been set up, at the end of each fiscal year the terminal year should be advanced another year. In this way a college will always be looking ahead at least five or preferably ten years.

Now and then a Catholic administrator has questioned the value of a ten-year or even a five-year budget, because of the difficulty of getting a commitment from the major superiors of a Religious Community for any long period of time, because of their preoccupation with other financial problems of the Community, and because of the dislike of seeming to bind a succeeding administration.

There is a difficulty here, no doubt, but the writer does not believe that it is insuperable. In any event, the drafting of a ten-

---

[2] The Fund for the Advancement of Education, established by the Ford Foundation, has done much to educate for and to advance long-range planning.

ear budget is a worthwhile endeavor in itself, even though it does not get the full encouragement of the religious high command. The ability to draft such a budget is a real test of the adequacy of the college's bookkeeping and accounting procedures.[3] As a technique it can have great educational value for officers of administration. It can contribute to more meaningful management of the material resources of the institution. It is invaluable, if not indispensable, in planning an intelligent development program.

[3] A how-to-do-it manual, prepared under the direction of the Commission on College Finance of the Association of American Colleges and financed by a grant from the United States Steel Foundation, is expected to be published in 1965.

CHAPTER 14

Endowments and Trust Funds

IN GENERAL the term "endowment fund" refers to monies set aside for investment with the understanding that the principal of the fund itself shall remain intact and only the income shall be used for the purposes established when the fund was set up. Endowment funds are classified as restricted if the income can be used only for certain specified purposes as, for example, for scholarships or student loan purposes or, as in the case of the Ford Foundation grants to colleges, for improving faculty salaries. Endowment funds are classified as unrestricted if the institution has complete freedom in the use of the income. An endowment fund may be restricted for a definite period of time and thereafter unrestricted as to income or even as to principal. In the latter case the inviolability of the principal may be terminated so that all or part of the principal may be expended, depending of course upon the terms set down by the donor. The Ford Foundation grants to colleges for improving faculty salaries furnish an example of this type of endowment fund. After a period of ten years, according to the terms of the grant, a college may use the principal sum in any way that it sees fit. In all of these matters there is the element of "trust," in that a college must observe the terms set by the donor of the funds.

The term "trust fund" is usually applied to monies (or the equivalent) held and administered by a responsible agent or trustee for the benefit of a particular person, group, institution, or activity. Thus a man may leave his estate in trust with a responsible person or bank for the benefit of his children, until they reach a certain age. Another may bequeath his estate to a college with the proviso that it be held in trust by a bank for his wife so that she may have the income during her lifetime. Only after her death is the capital sum to be paid over unconditionally to the college. In all these instances there is at least the implied doubt as to the ability of the children or the wife to manage the estate and to carry out the will of the donor, and so there is a third party involved and a written trust agreement which spells out the donor's wishes and the conditions of the trust. A college is considered capable of managing funds given to it for specified purposes, and outside third parties are only occasionally involved as trustees.

As far as colleges are concerned, there is a real distinction between endowment funds and trust funds. But in the case of the small Catholic college which does not have substantial endowment funds, the writer believes that there is much to be said for voluntarily making use of the trust fund idea for the safeguarding and management of permanent endowment funds. It will be the purpose of this chapter to explain this idea.

CATHOLIC COLLEGES AND ENDOWMENT FUNDS

Very few Catholic colleges can report anything substantial in the way of funded endowments. In the past, it is true, many Catholic college administrators were very little concerned with establishing endowment funds. They were more anxious to get funds for necessary building and expansion and for paying off debts. The possibility of raising funds for long-term purposes, investing these funds, and using only the income seemed to be impracticable. Against the funded endowments of other colleges, Catholic colleges have balanced their endowment of contributed services. This has been a great asset to Catholic colleges, to be sure, but its relative value has declined steadily with the growth of these colleges, the relative decrease in the number of Religious personnel, the corresponding increase in the number of lay personnel, and the rapidly rising cost of operating colleges. In the days when the faculty was almost completely staffed by members of a Religious Community, there was some justification for a feeling of security and complacency. But those days are gone forever. Catholic colleges now lament the fact that they lack the endowment funds for general and special purposes which are possessed by most non-Catholic colleges. In appealing for funds today they expressly include provisions for endowment.

It is true that many Catholic colleges now carry on their books a grant from the Ford Foundation under the stipulation that for a ten-year period the principal shall be invested and the income therefrom used to improve faculty salaries. This is not necessarily a permanent endowment because after the ten-year period the college has the unrestricted use of the principal sum.

CUSTODY OF ENDOWMENT FUNDS

Some Catholic colleges are unsophisticated in the use and custody of endowment funds. In part this is understandable because they have had little experience in dealing with them. Funds given to Catholic colleges in the past to support scholarships or awards of one type or another in perpetuity have not always been treated as endowment funds.

Instead of investing such funds in interest-bearing securities, keeping the principal intact and using only the income, colleges have often expended the principal on buildings and improvements and financed the scholarship obligation out of current revenue. This is an improvident and short-sighted policy that should not be countenanced. In accepting permanent scholarship funds a college should keep the principal inviolate and use the income only. Incidentally, it is not likely that a college will repeat today the mistake sometimes made in the past of assuring a prospective donor that a fixed sum, say $10,000, will guarantee a full scholarship in perpetuity, or that half the amount will support a tuition scholarship!

TRUST OBLIGATIONS

Whenever funds are given to a college with the understanding that the principal is to be kept intact, or more important still, if a benefaction is left to the college as a bequest in a will under a similar stipulation, there is both a legal and a moral obligation that the principal be held inviolate. Even the investment of such funds at a fixed rate of interest in income-producing buildings of a college has long been frowned upon, although some relaxation is to be noted today. It is still not good policy nor is it recommended practice because of the danger, no matter how remote, of losing sight of the fact that these monies are held in trust.

MANAGING ENDOWMENTS

Large colleges and universities, which have millions of dollars in investment funds, are very careful to segregate the management of these funds from the ordinary operations of the treasurer's office. The investment of endowment funds is usually handled through a separate office under the charge of a highly competent official. A constant watch is kept on the investment portfolio so as to insure for the institution the highest possible return on the invested funds, while the security of the principal, which is of paramount importance, is safeguarded.

The average small college, and especially the Catholic College, does not have the specialized facilities to handle investments, the safeguarding of securities and such matters. This becomes one of the chores of the treasurer's office or the business office. Fortunately, outside help is readily available. Lay members of the Board of Trustees or the Associated Board can frequently be of great help to a college in advising on the investment and custody of these funds. As a general rule the writer favors making use of the management and custodial services of a reputable trust company, or trust department of a recognized bank, under a legally executed Trust Agreement between the college and the bank.

In examining auditors' annual reports on small colleges, it is always interesting to read the statements dealing with the invested funds and to note the relationship between the book value and market value of the stocks and bonds in the investment portfolio. Even though only a few hundred thousand dollars is involved—and this is the usual situation with Catholic colleges—it is interesting to see whether the total market value of the securities exceeds the book value or the book value exceeds the market value. Invariably one finds that the colleges with appreciated investments are getting outside advice while those with depreciated investments are getting no outside help.

THE TRUST FUND AGREEMENT

The "Trust Fund Agreement" to which we refer is a legal document which binds both the college and the trust company. It is irrevocable by nature unless expressly declared to be revocable. It should be drawn up with great care and should have the benefit of the advice of the legal counsel of the college. Such a trust fund agreement should have at least the following provisions: (1) It should set forth the terms and conditions of the trust with sufficient flexibility to take care not only of present needs but also of future and unforeseen contingencies. (2) It should provide for some college voice in the investments, either in the form of approval or a veto privilege. (3) It should provide for pooling the funds of the trust with other similar trust funds of the college for investment purposes. (4) It should provide, where this is possible, for freedom under state laws that might harmfully narrow down the area of investments. (5) It should specify the manner of paying income. (6) It should make provision for the proper recording of the names of donors and any restrictions which they may have stipulated on the use of funds.

ADVANTAGES OF CUSTODIAL SERVICES

The handling of endowment funds through trust agreements, as advocated, is more than worth the moderate charge, usually based on a percentage of the income earned. Among the advantages to be secured by turning over funds to the management of a recognized bank or trust company are the following: (1) The funds are segregated from other college funds and are permanently dedicated to the purposes for which they were originally intended. Thus the danger of using the funds in an emergency for other purposes is avoided. (2) Banks and trust companies have the facilities for handling the investment of such funds, the collection of income, and the safeguarding of the securities which represent the investment. (3) Regular reports, which will be forthcoming at stated intervals, will simplify the bookkeeping problem and insure that proper records are kept. The dates for submitting these reports can be arranged to tie in with the fiscal year of the college. (4) Prospective donors have more reason for confidence in the college and will be more likely to give funds for various endowment purposes.

Although the business officer of the college is freed from much of the worry and responsibility which attaches to endowment funds, the college is not freed from all responsibility. Thus the treasurer's office ought to maintain in separate folders a complete record of each trust fund with all the relevant correspondence and information. There should be a small finance committee of the Board of Trustees to approve the investments suggested by the trust company. This committee might be composed of the president and the treasurer of the college, together with a lay member of the board who has had some investment experience. Such a committee may wish from time to time to suggest new investments to the trust company, since in any case both parties must approve.

Examples of Trust Agreements

It is greatly to be desired that the college have the final say in the wording of any trust agreement. Particularly is this the case when a prospective benefactor is involved. For this reason it is advisable that a college have standard forms of trust agreements which have been approved by the Board of Trustees of the college and which can be submitted to prospective benefactors.

Two types of such trust agreements are usually sufficient: one to cover the general corporate purposes of the institution, so that the income may be added to current funds or used in any way the trustees of the college may approve; and one to cover special purposes such as scholarships, awards, professorships, etc. Two such sample agreements follow:

TRUST AGREEMENT FOR GENERAL CORPORATE PURPOSES

WHEREAS, on the eighth day of July A.D. 1964, we, THE SMITH-TOWN TRUST COMPANY did receive from MYTHICAL COLLEGE of the STATE OF JACKSON, the sum of One Hundred Thousand Dollars ($100,000.00) to be held in TRUST to establish a Fund to be known as MYTHICAL COLLEGE ENDOWMENT FUND under the following terms and conditions.

IN TRUST, to invest, reinvest and manage the same with the approval of the duly elected representatives of the Board of Trustees of MYTHICAL COLLEGE and to pay the net income thereof semi-annually to the said College for its general and special corporate purposes.

It is expressly understood that the parties hereto do not wish to limit themselves to so-called "legal investments" if, in their judgment, other investments are preferable.

It is also understood that in order to provide greater security of principal and uniformity of income, the principal funds of this TRUST may for investment purposes be pooled with other similar Trust Funds of the said College under the Trusteeship of the SMITHTOWN TRUST COMPANY.

And be it further understood that a schedule shall be kept with the records of this Trust, showing the name or names of donors together with the amount of their benefactions.

IN WITNESS WHEREOF, we have hereunto set our hands and corporate seals this twelfth day of July A.D. 1964.

> The SMITHTOWN TRUST COMPANY
> (Signed) J. Winkle, President
> Attest: F. Smith, Secretary
> MYTHICAL COLLEGE of the
> STATE OF JACKSON
> (Signed) John White, President
> Attest: A. Black, Secretary

TRUST AGREEMENT FOR SPECIAL CORPORATE PURPOSES
(A Scholarship Fund)

WHEREAS, on the eighth day of July A.D. 1964, we, THE SMITH-TOWN TRUST COMPANY did receive from MYTHICAL COLLEGE of the STATE OF JACKSON, the sum of Ten Thousand Dollars ($10,000.00), to be held in TRUST to establish a Scholarship to be known as the JULES PRINGLE SCHOLARSHIP under the following terms and conditions.

IN TRUST, to invest, reinvest and manage the same with the approval of the duly elected representatives of the Board of Trustees of MYTHICAL COLLEGE and to pay the net income thereof semi-annually to the said College for the maintenance of a scholarship for a worthy and deserving student, the same to be selected and appointed by the President of said College from time to time. Payment is to be made to the said College upon presentation by it of a certificate setting forth that a student has been appointed and was duly registered and assigned to this Scholarship.

It is expressly understood that the parties hereto do not wish to limit themselves to so-called "legal investments" if, in their judgment, other investments seem preferable.

It is also understood that in order to provide greater security of principal and uniformity of income, the principal funds of this Trust may for investment purposes be pooled with other similar Trust Funds of MYTHICAL COLLEGE under the Trusteeship of the SMITH-TOWN TRUST COMPANY.

IN WITNESS WHEREOF, we have hereunto set our hands and corporate seals this twelfth day of July A.D. 1964.

> The SMITHTOWN TRUST COMPANY
> (Signed) J. Winkle, President
> Attest: F. Smith, Secretary
> MYTHICAL COLLEGE of the
> STATE OF JACKSON
> (Signed) John White, President
> Attest: A. Black, Secretary

RAISING ENDOWMENT FUNDS

The raising of scholarship funds has an appeal to both alumni and students. Local alumni clubs can be encouraged to feel that in each instance the fund is peculiarly their own. They can begin the fund with a modest amount and add to it year by year. Individual members can contribute to such a fund, or it can be made the objective of money raising social events. The raising of scholarship funds will also appeal to students in the various college classes. Such funds can be set up under trust at the end of the freshman year out of the surplus funds raised by a class social affair. No matter how small this beginning, there is an incentive to add to it during the succeeding years at college. The good accomplished by such funds is a vital one that continues from year to year. Directly or indirectly these funds are investments in promising young men and young women, who are thus helped to prepare themselves more effectively for service to God and country and fellowmen. The raising of these endowments for scholarships will also be a way of easing the drain on current income for the many Catholic colleges which must provide a great part of scholarship allowances out of current funds.

Permanent endowment funds for scholarships, student loans, and other needs of a college appeal to some prospective donors who would not contribute to new buildings, to the purchase of equipment, to improvements in grounds and buildings or similar special projects. They will contribute to endowment funds for general purposes or for such special purposes as scholarships, loan funds, professorships and awards of one type or another, either by outright gifts or by making bequest provisions in their wills. Particularly is this true when it is known that such funds will carry the names of the donors or of the persons whose memories they intend to commemorate, and that these names will regularly be mentioned in the printed literature of the college. These funds make very suitable permanent memorials for the living as well as the departed. The fact that they constitute independent trusts and may not be converted for use in other ways is actually a good talking point in the solicitation of such funds.

From small acorns large oak trees grow. In similar fashion, from very modest beginnings college endowment funds can grow to sizable proportions over the years. But if there is no small acorn there can be no lordly oak.

CHAPTER 15

Financial Support
from the Religious Community

VERY FEW Catholic colleges could have survived up to the present
without the generous help of the Religious Communities which
operate most of them, or without the help of the dioceses which
sponsor the dozen diocesan colleges. This help consists of both
"contributed services" and direct or indirect cash subsidies. By
contributed services we mean, of course, the net value to the
college of the services of the Religious or the diocesan clergy
after their subsistence allowances have been deducted. By cash
subsidies we mean actual financial help given to the college. This
is probably much more generous and sustained on the part of
Religious Communities than on the part of the few dioceses
which sponsor colleges. In this chapter we will be concerned
chiefly with the colleges operated by Religious Communities
which comprise about ninety-five percent of all Catholic colleges.

With the possible exception of the newer colleges, very few
Catholic colleges could begin to compute the *total* value of the
past cash subsidies of the Religious Communities, to say nothing
of the monetary value of the services of the Religious who have
staffed the colleges. It has been literally true that Religious
Communities, in the past, have "not counted the cost" of their
colleges. Like generous parents they have neither kept a careful

136

record of the actual cash expended on their offspring nor put any monetary value on the services rendered to them.

CHANGED CONDITIONS

Conditions are quite different today. The operation of colleges has become so expensive that contributed services and other subsidies from Religious Communities can no longer absorb operating deficits, much less provide capital funds for expansion and development. Fortunately help is now available from several other sources on a "show cause basis." But it is up to the particular college to demonstrate that support is being given by those who have close association with the college. Certainly Religious Communities come under this category, along with students, parents, and graduates.

All financial help received by a college should be reflected in its financial statements. In the financial accounting of Catholic colleges and universities it is the generally accepted practice to take full monetary account of the contributed services and other financial subsidies of the Religious Community. Otherwise the financial statements of Catholic colleges would not be fully comparable to those of other colleges and universities. Accrediting associations, government agencies, and all who require comparable financial statements expect this. It would be a great disservice to a Catholic college to ignore or discount the cash value of the contributed services of the Religious who staff the college, or to lose sight of the direct or indirect subsidies given to a college by the motherhouse or headquarters of the Religious Community. By the same token it helps neither Religious Community nor college to refrain from giving a cash value to whatever educational or noneducational services a college may render to the Religious Community.

There may be a certain amount of reluctance on the part of the average Religious to put a cash value on the service which he renders in the first place to God. Some may even feel annoyance at the idea of evaluating the services and fiscal relations of a Religious Community on a strictly businesslike basis. But this manner of accounting is necessary and serves a good purpose.

The reporting of such contributions in terms of actual cash value does not mean that one ignores the spiritual motivation for the labor and self-sacrifice involved.

COMPENSATING SERVICES OF RELIGIOUS

Religious should be compensated in accordance with the same salary scale which applies to lay members of the faculty. If Sister Joan, Ph.D., a full-time member of the faculty with the rank of professor, dedicates her services to the college, the gross value of her services will be equivalent to whatever is paid a lay professor for comparable services, or would be paid if there were a lay professor of similar rank and seniority. In default of both these guides, recourse can be had to average salary payments reported for similar colleges in the same section of the country.

But what should be done with the substantial royalty payments which Sister Joan receives from the sale of her book and with the honorarium which she received from her lecture before the Business Women's Club? Here one must distinguish between personal or "family" income and college income. What would happen to the royalty income of Professor Smith and to the lecture fees which he occasionally receives? Is it not considered personal income, a sort of bonus which he no doubt welcomes for his family's sake? Certainly the college has no claim to this income nor is it offset by any deduction from his salary. In similar fashion there is no reason for the college treasury to lay claim to the extra income of Sister Joan. Of course she has a vow of poverty. But this does not mean that money which comes to her personally should go to the college. Actually money that comes to her personally, whatever its source, belongs to her "family," the Religious Community, not to the college.

If income proper to the Religious Community is deposited in the college treasury as current income, the financial report of the college will not be strictly comparable to that of other colleges. Nevertheless, the income which does not belong to the college and which goes directly to the Religious Community may be of indirect benefit to the college. Presumably this money will be used to help pay the expenses of the Religious Community. In this event more money will be returned to the college by way of donation, or the net value of contributed services will be greater.

Methods of Accounting for Services

Accounting fully for the services of Religious personnel can be accomplished in one of three ways: (1) by paying full salaries to the Religious Community; (2) on a bookkeeping basis only, by recording the lay equivalent salary of the Religious as an expense with a contra credit to contributed service income; (3) by paying partial salaries to the Religious Community with the balance recorded as an expense with a contra credit to contributed service income. Any one of these methods can satisfy the need for accurate accounting. It is up to the individual college to adopt the method which meets its needs or has greatest appeal.

1. *Paying Full Salaries.*   Salaries can be paid in full for Religious personnel on exactly the same basis as for lay personnel. In this event, just as laymen must pay for personal and family expenses out of their salaries, so the Religious Community, which receives the monthly salary checks for the Religious, must pay the equivalent expenses of the Religious. The college is reimbursed by check for whatever services it may supply, such as board and room, for example. After all expenses of the Religious Community have been taken care of, the remainder may be paid to the college as a donation or grant from the Religious Community and should be so recorded. In this instance there are no "contributed services" in the accepted meaning of this phrase. Instead, there is a direct cash subsidy from the Religious Community.

For external purposes there is no reason to make any distinction in a financial report between the salaries paid to Religious and to lay faculty. For internal purposes, however, there would have to be a distinction between Religious and lay salaries because part of the former may be given back to the college as a donation. Therefore, the relationship between Religious and lay salaries would be an important item for financial planning.

This method of paying full salaries requires that there be no delays on the part of the Religious Community in making the agreed reimbursements and subsidy payments to the college.

Otherwise the college could be financially embarrassed. This is a reason why this method is not acceptable to some colleges. From an accounting point of view the method is good. It emphasizes the voluntary character of the donations of the Religious Community and it keeps the record straight. In this direct salary method there would be no reason to claim the equivalent of an "endowment value" for the services of the Religious. If, however, the Religious Community is willing to guarantee to the college an annual donation of a stated amount, this could be pointed to as an equivalent to the income from an endowment fund of a certain estimated amount.

2. *A Bookkeeping Transaction.* Under this method the services of Religious are strictly accounted for on a salary basis, and the college is reimbursed for whatever expenditures are made for the Religious Community or its members. But all this is accomplished through bookkeeping transactions. The total salaries of Religious are debited to "expense" and the contributed service account is credited by a bookkeeping entry. Any expenses of the Religious paid for by the college are charged against the contributed service account, so that the resulting figure is the "net" value of the contributed services to the college and is considered as income. The charges against contributed services for expenses of the Religious may be accumulated in a separate account or accounts if desired. No money is actually transferred. This is one form of "contributed services."

Although this method takes full account of contributed services it is not a clean operation from an accounting point of view. Since there is no separation between college funds and Religious Community funds, there are no cancelled checks to show for partial salary payments to the Religious Community; and the Religious Community does not pay with its own checks for the personal expenses of the Religious. All of these personal or "family" expenses are subject, therefore, to the review of the auditors although, strictly speaking, they do not pertain to the college any more than do the personal expenditures which a lay faculty member makes from his faculty salary.

3. *Part Payment, Part Bookkeeping.* This third method is a combination of methods one and two. By agreement between

Religious Community and college, part of the salaries for the Religious is paid by check to the Religious Community. This payment should be sufficient to enable the Religious Community to defray all expenses of the Religious Community and all personal expenses of the Religious, including reimbursement to the college for whatever services and subsistence it may supply—for example, board and lodging. All transactions should be by bank check. The balance of the salaries which remain with the college after these part payments, constitute the net value to the college of the "contributed services."

In this case also, total salaries may be recorded by a bookkeeping entry with contra credit to contributed services. Payments to the Religious Community are charged to the contributed services account, or to a separate account which is subsequently deducted from the contributed services account.

This is a preferred form of "contributed services." It has none of the disadvantages which could be associated with the first form. It provides a clean accounting record because all transactions are by check. It permits the Religious Community to pay directly for all personal expenses of its members, thus removing all these "family matters from the purview of the auditors who will be interested only in the cancelled checks as partial-salary payments to the Religious Community. All things considered, this appeals to the author as the best method to account for contributed services.

CHARGES AND DEDUCTIONS

The choice of the method by which a college is to account for the monetary value of the services of its Religious personnel does not automatically solve the problem of accounting for these services. One reason for this is that the individual Religious receives no money himself for his services, and ordinarily pays out no money for his own subsistence. He is not apt to be conscious of what should or should not be charged against him. A lay member, on the contrary, is very conscious of his actual salary, his "take-home" pay, and his expenses. If there is anything added or omitted, he will be quick to report this. He will make certain that he is reimbursed for any expenses which he believes the college ought to assume. There is no chance in the world that his book royalties, payments for his articles, stipends for his services as a guest lecturer, etc. will be considered current income of the college.

Furthermore, the business office of a college is accustomed to dealing with lay personnel on a more or less businesslike basis. Before monthly salary checks are paid out there are deductions to be made for social security, retirement annuity premiums, hospitalization insurance and the like. If a lay member has arranged with the business office for certain purchases to be made for his home, he will expect the college to bill him for this, or he may ask the business office to deduct this from his next paycheck. In any event there is no danger that these items will be overlooked.

The college administration has to have more sensitivity as to what is, or what is not, a legitimate deduction or charge against the salaries of Religious, than would be the case with lay members of the faculty. And there must also be sensitivity as to what constitutes income of the Religious Community rather than income of the college. At least in the beginning it may seem a little more difficult to figure out what should be considered personal and "family" expenses of Religious. But it does not take long to become accustomed to this.

Fortunately there is a convenient rule of thumb for settling most of the questions that arise in computing the value of the services of Religious to a college. With but few exceptions all Catholic colleges now have large numbers of salaried personnel. This provides a comparative basis on which the answers to questions can be made. Whenever there is doubt as to whether something is or is not a charge against the salary of a religious, the question should be phrased as if it applied to a lay professor and the proper answer ought to come out. This is based on the assumption that, since both lay teacher and Religious teacher are credited on the books with similar salaries, both ought to be treated alike in all matters that impinge on salaries. Ordinarily a lay professor is expected, for example, to furnish or to pay for such things as meals, lodging, clothing, medical care, transportation, vacations, and all such personal items. For the Religious faculty member these same expenses are charges against the salary of the Religious, whether the bills are paid directly by the Religious Community or by the college.

It may be objected that in many instances a strict application of this principle of impartiality would not be quite fair to the Religious teacher. For example, it is college policy to absorb the expenses of a faculty member only when he attends a scholarly or professional meeting as the official representative of the college, or when he appears on the program of the meeting as a chairman, speaker, discussant, or officer of the association concerned. Furthermore, any lay faculty member who wishes to attend the meetings can go at his own expense, if he can make the necessary arrangements for classes. But the Religious faculty member is sometimes said to be at a disadvantage because receiving no salary payments directly, he or she is not in a position personally to pay expenses for attending the meeting.

To this the reply can be made that the Religious really is not at a disadvantage when it comes to attending these meetings. Although the college cannot directly pay his expenses if he falls outside the policy limitation, the Religious Community can and should pay the expenses if he wishes to attend the meeting. Actually the expenses would be paid out of the salary or part-salary payments which the Religious Community is entitled to draw from the college.

When the Religious faculty of a college has its own residence and separate kitchen and dining facilities, there is no problem in keeping living expenses of the Religious distinct from the college. Whatever expense the college may incur in furnishing utilities like water, heat, gas, light, power or other services, can readily be charged to and paid by the Religious Community. But when there is joint use of certain facilities, a floor or wing of a college building, a common kitchen and so on, expenses have to be estimated and pro-rated on some equitable basis. When there is doubt about an allocation of charges there need be no scruple in resolving the doubt in favor of the Religious Community. This is justified because there are many intangible services rendered to a college outside the call of duty, for which a Religious Community can never be fully compensated.

There may be other adjustments to be made. Thus, if a college furnished lunch or other meals without charge to lay members of the faculty, this should apply also to the Religious faculty members. If a young lay instructor would be given room and board in return for services as a proctor in a student dormitory, the same arrangement should apply to a Religious who performs this service. In both cases, of course, cash values ought to be attached to these perquisites.

There are some instances where this "rule of thumb" method does not readily apply. Thus the salaries of Religious, whether paid directly to their Community or left with the college, are not subject to withholding for income tax purposes. On the other hand, the so-called "fringe benefits" enjoyed by lay faculty members introduce some situations which are not readily comparable. There are no T.I.A.A. (retirement annuity) contributions or Social Security payments for Religious. Should one endeavor to equalize the situation for Religious (or even lay-teachers) who have no children to send to college tuition-free? These are problems that one can try to work out equitably. For our purpose, however, the underlying principle does not change: What applies to the lay teacher ought to apply in a similar way to the Religious teacher in the same college, and vice-versa.

AN OVERSIGHT

A source of contributed services, sometimes overlooked, occurs when a college is served on a full-time basis by diocesan clergy or by members of a Religious Community other than that which operates the college. Rarely do these faculty members receive a cash compensation equal to that of the lay faculty members. Their actual compensation may be considerably below the comparable value of their services. This differential should be computed on the same basis as the contributed services of the Religious Community which operates the college.

The college which pays full salaries to its own Religious, and therefore feels that it has no contributed services, may readily overlook this source of contributed services. But it is just as likely to be overlooked by the college which recognizes contributed services as bookkeeping procedure or as a part-payment, part-bookkeeping procedure.

One provincial superior, whose subjects are regularly assigned as teachers in colleges operated by other Religious Communities, makes explicit allowances for contributed service. In the written agreement covering these services it is specified that the Religious assigned to the college shall be granted rank and promotion in rank, in accordance with the established policies of the institution and on a par with other teachers at that institution. They are also to be credited with a salary that is appropriate to their rank, training and experience. From this salary the college is asked to deduct a fixed percentage which is to be credited to contributed services. Then after deducting such personal expenses as these Religious may have incurred, the balance is forwarded to their Community.

GROSS AND NET VALUES

When the "contributed services" method is used to account for the services of Religious personnel it is necessary to make a distinction between the *gross* and *net* value of these services. (This necessity does not arise when Religious are compensated on a full salary basis.)

The *gross* value to a college of the contributed services of the Religious for a month or for a fiscal year is the sum total of the salaries credited to the Religious for that month or that fiscal year, without any deductions. This would also be the case with a lay faculty member or a maintenance employee if the college had supplied him, for example, with room and board. The value of this service would be included in his *gross* salary but would not appear in his *net* or take-home pay. This procedure is necessary for the proper allocation of salary expenses to the various accounts, such as departments of instruction, offices of administration, library, maintenance, and so on. If only the net value of these contributed services were used, the result would not be truly comparable to the college with only salaried lay employees. For a similar reason, whenever it is necessary to report, on a comparable basis, the total payroll of the college, or its academic payroll, the figures for the gross value of contributed services should always be used.

The *net* value to a college of the contributed services of Religious for a month or for a fiscal year is found by charging against the contributed services account for that month or that fiscal year all legitimate deductions. An example of such a deduction would be, of course, the part-salary payment made to the Religious Community. Whenever any personal needs of the Religious as, for example, lodging and meals are supplied by the college, and the college is not reimbursed for this by the Religious Community, then this expense would also be a deduction from the contributed services account. If the Religious Community receives no part-salary payments and the college pays for all personal expenses of the Religious, these would all be deductions. In brief, the net value to a college of the contributed services is that part of the total contribution of the Religious which remains after such appropriate deductions have been made. It is only the net value of these services, the equivalent of take-home pay, which has a cash value to the college.

ACCOUNTING MEMORANDA

In reporting salaries of Religious, external agencies such as accrediting associations, government agencies, foundations, and the like usually want no distinction made between contributed services and paid salaries unless they specifically request a distinction. But in reporting salary items it might be clearer to write: "salaries, including contributed services." If Religious are paid full salaries there is, of course, no distinction of any kind to be made.

For internal purposes—for the administration, for the board of trustees and for the Religious Community—a distinction should always be made between the salaries of Religious personnel, whether fully paid or considered as contributed services, and the salaries of lay personnel. This is important for financial planning, as was pointed out before, and for budgetary and other administrative purposes.

The author has seen college financial reports prepared by various auditing firms which make it easy to use one financial report for both external and internal purposes. This is readily possible when lay salaries and Religious salaries (or contributed services) are sub-totaled as illustrated below under Library Expenses.

LIBRARY EXPENSES

Salaries		
Lay	$ 6,500.00	
Religious (or contributed services)	12,300.00	$18,800.00
Book purchases		6,700.00
Periodicals		918.00
Binding		804.00
Supplies and expenses		516.00
Total		$27,738.00

Whenever the services of Religious are applicable, whether in Administration, Instruction, Bookstore, Cafeteria, Maintenance, or anything else, the statements of expense for each should be treated in the manner illustrated for the Library. Again, when analyzing expenditures by classification, the salary item can head a double column to provide for "lay" and "Religious" salaries, or "cash" and "contributed" salaries as the case may be.

When the method of contributed services is used to account for the services of Religious, the author believes that the current *net* value of these services should be regularly mentioned in the auditor's report. Since the net value of these services is a regular and continuous contribution to the college, its endowment value can be readily calculated. This information deserves a place on the balance sheet of the college in the form of a prominent foot-note somewhat as follows:

For the fiscal year 19_____ - 19_____the services contributed to.................College by the Sisters of...... ....had a net value to the College of $200,000.00. At a conservative interest rate of 4% this amount is the equivalent of the income for one year from an endowment fund of $5,000,000.00.

The total net value of contributed services should also appear on the Summary Income Statement as a separate heading following "Gifts and Grants." This will minimize the danger of mis-interpreting the total "Educational and General Income." This contributed service is one of the items which helps to balance the educational deficit.

OTHER SUPPORT FROM THE RELIGIOUS COMMUNITY

In addition to the contributed services of the Religious, whether in the form of donations or bookkeeping credits, Religious Communities have helped their colleges through various other forms of support. Sometimes a Religious Community has continuously subsidized a college to enable it to meet its current operating expenses. Sometimes it gives outright gifts for building purposes or for mortgage liquidation. In some instances loans are made without any interest obligation. Instances are known where the motherhouse corporation of a Religious Community has assumed all the mortgage debt of a college, including payments on interest and principal, in order that the college itself may be freed from this burden. In other instances, especially where college and motherhouse are adjoining institutions, building and facilities, built and owned by the motherhouse corporation, have been made available for use by the college, rent-free.

Certainly these Religious Communities are deserving of the highest commendation for the great sacrifices they have made in supporting their colleges. Few, if any of the diocesan colleges have been able to command anything like a comparable measure of support from the sponsoring dioceses. But proper accounting records are important.

In suggesting that the support of the college be carried out in such a way that the donors can justly be recognized and the college can be given credit for paying its just debts, there is no intention to find fault with the support of the Religious communities for their colleges or to minimize that support. It is important that the legitimate expenses and debts of a college be a matter of record on its books, no matter who supplies the wherewithal to meet them. It is also important that the Religious Community gets proper credit for its benefactions to the college, and that the college gets proper credit for the value of its services to the Religious Community.

A college must correctly record all its income and expenses if the real cost of its operations is to be reflected on its books. This would mean, for example, that if the Religious Community wishes to make the interest or principal payments on a college mortgage, the way to do this is to send the check to the college where it can be credited as a donation. Then let the college make the interest or principal payments with its own check. In this way the legitimate expense will be correctly reflected on its books. If the motherhouse corporation wishes to make physical facilities available to a college, let the motherhouse receive a fair rental for the facilities used, even if this would mean that the motherhouse must donate sufficient money to the college to pay the rental.

If a college educates Sisters of its own Religious Community, it should receive an actual cash payment for these services, based on the tuition charges and fees which apply to clergy and Religious of other Communities. It is misleading, if not improper, to charge this tuition to scholarship expense, as is sometimes done. If the Religious Community feels that it cannot afford the additional drain on its resources, let it collect more of the salary of the Religious who teach in the college and then pay it back in tuition. In this way neither college nor Religious Community will be made richer or poorer by the transaction, but the account books of both will be straight.

An approximate *quid pro quo* arrangement whereby the motherhouse corporation makes available certain facilities rent free, or pays the interest on the mortgage in return for the education, tuition free, of junior Sisters, novices or postulants, is not satisfactory. It may happen that nothing appears on the record; even if it did, this is not the businesslike way of doing things that is expected of a modern college. If the motherhouse actually paid the college for these services in cash, the college could then pay the rent or the interest on the mortgage. This would keep the records of both motherhouse and college on a businesslike basis. Unless these simple fiscal procedures are observed, it is not possible for the financial statement of a college to be strictly accurate. Nor will it be possible for the financial report to be fully comparable with the reports of other colleges.

THE QUESTION OF DIOCESAN SUPPORT

There are those who think that some form of diocesan support is becoming increasingly necessary for colleges, and that Religious Communities cannot be expected to carry the full burden as in the past. They point to what has happened on the secondary school level. For many years Religious Communities were expected to carry the burden of secondary education almost alone. Now it is being recognized more and more that the financing of these schools is pretty much a diocesan responsibility. It is also pointed out that many Protestant colleges are receiving increasingly generous yearly support from their sponsoring church bodies.

The writer sees no hope in the foreseeable future for any regular financial help from the Church comparable to what is being received by Protestant colleges. The example of the Protestant churches is not really apposite, since most of these churches do not have a widespread system of primary and secondary schools to support. Furthermore, direct financial help from the Church on a regular basis has not been given even to the diocesan Catholic colleges which are directly sponsored by dioceses of the Church.

It is true that a few colleges conducted by Religious Communities have received occasional grants of funds from a diocese of the Catholic Church. This has been particularly true of some of the more recent colleges which were being established in areas where no previous Catholic colleges existed. But these few instances can hardly be considered to set a precedent. The fact is that only one out of 250 Catholic colleges and universities currently receives regular financial support from the Church. That support, which is relatively modest, is on a national basis, provided through a yearly collection taken up in all or most of the dioceses of the Catholic Church in the United States.

CHAPTER 16

A Public Financial Statement

COLLEGES HAVE no hesitation today in admitting they have financial problems. Despite sizable increases, tuition charges cover only part of the cost of instruction. This has always been more or less true. But with rising costs greatly outstripping possible increases in tuition, all colleges have educational deficits and are, in a sense, proud of it. When the educational and general expenses of a college are measured against income from student tuition and fees, there is bound to be a deficit. No one is surprised or embarrassed. If in comparing these two totals, a college statement showed a net surplus, this would be a source of amazement —if it did not raise doubts as to the accuracy of the entire statement. As a consequence, very few Catholic colleges today hesitate to admit educational deficits or to reveal their financial problems.

Along with other colleges and universities, Catholic colleges rightly believe that they are operating in the public interest and are deserving of a measure of help from the general public. They make no apologies in appealing to parents, alumni, friends, corporations and foundations for assistance in making up deficits and raising teachers' salaries. They do not hesitate to point out that capital expenditures for buildings and equipment are just not possible without generous gifts and bequests from wealthy individuals, without substantial help from alumni, friends and the general public, and without long-term, low-interest loans.

SECRECY IN THE PAST

It was not always thus. In the past comparatively few Catholic colleges made their financial reports generally available. Why not? Probably because it had never been done before. Most Catholic colleges are operated by Religious Communities which have been very hesitant to share their financial problems with "outsiders." It would have been embarrassing if other Religious Communities, or the general public, knew that the college had operating deficits and was dependent on subsidies from the province or motherhouse to make the interest and principal payments on the mortgage.

Again, some accrediting agencies were inclined to look with disapproval on the college which, without visible financial endowment, bravely shouldered heavy debts and operated at a deficit. In some instances provinces or motherhouses assumed the debts and made interest and principal payments in order to remove the red ink from the college account books. But whatever may have been the story in the past, these days are gone or almost gone. The whole psychology of college financial operations has changed, and Catholic colleges are rending the veil of financial secrecy.

If the true financial situation of more Catholic colleges were made known to alumni, friends, and other members of the public interested in these colleges, not only would false ideas of their wealth be dissipated but greater voluntary support would be possible. It is high time that all Catholic colleges drop the traditional reticence about their financial affairs and take the public into their confidence.

FINANCIAL REPORTING PROCEDURES

Before a college publishes a financial statement for general distribution, there are certain fiscal and accounting practices that must first be adopted. Otherwise a statement would not be a "comparable financial statement," that is, one comparable to the financial statements issued by other colleges. Unless it is comparable, it may give misleading and erroneous impressions and thus do more harm than good. It is recommended that the following procedures be considered.

It would be difficult today to find a Catholic college which does not have an annual audit of its accounts and a financial report prepared by a firm of public accountants. This is now universal, largely because regional accrediting associations and other official agencies look for such reports. Also, prospective college borrowers have found that they will hardly get a hearing from banks, insurance companies or the Federal Government until there has been an opportunity to examine the college's financial report.

A college must make certain that the public accounting firm engaged to audit its books is familiar with college accounting procedures. It must insist that the financial report which the auditors prepare, observes the standard form and terminology recommended by *College and University Business Administration,* published by the American Council on Education. In college accounting, as contrasted with commercial accounting, the terms "profit" and "loss" are not used; "surplus" has a different connotation; depreciation of buildings, furnishings and equipment is not taken unless actually funded,[1] and so forth. One cannot always rest on the assurance that an auditing firm handles several college accounts. The author knows of three colleges which were served by the same auditing firm but had reports of three different types. Only one report followed the standard form and was satisfactory.

If the annual financial statements prepared by certified public accountants for a Catholic college are to be fully comparable

---

[1] There is no objection to supplementary records of depreciation or to mentioning it as a memorandum in the notes of an audit report. The calculation of depreciation on educational buildings and equipment will help to give the true cost of instruction. Making allowance for depreciation on property used by auxiliary enterprises and activities will aid in determining rates of fees and other charges. But this should not be a part of the regular financial report unless cash is set aside in replacement, or depreciation funds.

to those of non-Catholic colleges, the full monetary value (i.e., the salary equivalent) of services furnished by members of the Religious Community must be reflected in the accounting. Either proper allowance must be made for these contributed services, or the contributed services must be eliminated by paying for them through an actual cash transfer, as was explained in the preceding chapter.

There should be a clear-cut separation between the income and expenses of the local Religious Community as such, and the income and expenses of the college. Preferably this would mean a separate fund for the local Religious Community (a checking account would be sufficient), into which would be deposited all college salaries of the religious, or such portion of these salaries as is deemed necessary for the support of the Religious Community. Into this fund, administered by the Religious Superior of the local Community, would also go whatever money might accrue to a Religious for extra-collegiate activities, such as lectures, published articles, book royalties, tutoring, personal gifts, and so on. Also, in the case of priests, there would be Mass stipends, stipends for Sunday services, sermons, retreats, and so forth. Out of this fund should be paid all personal expenses of the Religious, such as board and room, clothing, medical and hospital care, travel for purposes other than college business, and the like. Where the college happens to furnish any of these services, reimbursement should be made by check from this Community fund. If there are assessments for the expenses of motherhouse or province, these should come not from the college but from the fund of the local Religious Community; and they should be provided from the salary payments of the Religious.

The preceding chapter dealt with fiscal relations between the college and the province or motherhouse of the Religious Community. These relations must also be on a strictly businesslike basis. For without sound fiscal policies between college and local Religious Community, and between college and the province or motherhouse of the Religious Community, it is not possible for a Catholic college to present a report that will be comparable to the financial reports of other colleges.

COMPILING THE FINANCIAL STATEMENT

Assuming that all these procedures of fiscal policy and accounting are being observed and that a certified public accountant's financial report for the college is available, we are ready to consider what ought to be comprised in the public financial statement which is to be made generally available.

In the first place the statement to be published ought to be brief and presented as simply as possible. Unless it can be read and understood, it will serve no purpose. It should consist essentially of a "Condensed Balance Sheet" as of the end of the most recent fiscal year, a "Summary of Current Income," and a "Summary of Current Expenditures,"—all for the same fiscal year.

If the auditor's financial report is in proper form, it should be possible for the college business manager to prepare the public statement readily from that report. Better still, once the auditor knows the form that is desired, he can prepare the statement along with his official report. In any event it is advantageous to have the name of the auditing firm attached in some way to the public statement. For this reason, even though the statement is prepared by the college business office from the auditor's report, it should have the auditor's specific approval. We shall briefly consider the three parts of the statement.

THE CONDENSED BALANCE SHEET

The Condensed Balance Sheet is intended to present in concise form the financial condition of the college, and of the funds for which the college is responsible, at a specified date. It is called "condensed" because it gives in shortened form information that is to be found in the auditor's report on one or more balance sheets with subsidiary or supporting statements.

The following fund groups are most commonly employed: Current Funds, Loan Funds, Endowment and Other Non-Expendable Funds, and Plant Funds. Other fund groups, such as Annuity Funds, Agency Funds, and the like may also be neces-

MYTHICAL COLLEGE
CONDENSED BALANCE SHEET
June 30, 1964

ASSETS		LIABILITIES	
I CURRENT FUNDS		**I CURRENT FUNDS**	
Cash	$ 39,513.10	Accounts payable	$ 16,800.85
Accounts receivable		Accrued payroll	3,748.60
(less bad debt allowance)	3,650.32	Prepaid fees, etc.	3,857.10
Inventories	15,800.60	Total liabilities	24,406.55
Prepaid expenses	4,748.85	Restricted funds	54,762.50
Investments	34,857.10	Current funds balance	19,400.92
Total	$ 98,569.97	Total	$ 98,569.97
II LOAN FUNDS		**II LOAN FUNDS**	
Cash	$ 5,734.00	Loan funds balances	
		U.S. Gov't. grant	$ 36,936.00
Loans receivable	35,306.00	College appropriation	4,104.00
Total	$ 41,040.00	Total	$ 41,040 00
III ENDOWMENT FUNDS		**III ENDOWMENT FUNDS**	
Cash	$ 26,730.50	Restricted principal	$ 217,200.50
Investments		Unrestricted principal	105,600.00
(Market val. $300,100.)	299,970.00	Reserve for losses	3,900.00
Total	$ 326,700.50	Total	$ 326,700.50
IV PLANT FUNDS		**IV PLANT FUNDS**	
A. Unexpended plant funds bal.	$ 260.98	A. Unexpended plant funds bal.	$ 260.98
B. Debt retirement funds bal.	3,000.00	B. Debt retirement funds bal.	3,000.00
C. Invested in plant		C. Invested in plant	
Land and improvements	334,650.00	Mortgage payable	343,249.40
Buildings	2,368,720.50	Bonds payable	998,660.00
Equipt. and furnishings	432,660.50	Net invested in plant	1,794,121.60
Total invested in plant	$3,136,031.00	Total invested in plant	$3,136,031.00
Total plant funds	$3,139,291.98	Total plant funds	$3,139,291.98
GRAND TOTAL	$3,605,602.45	GRAND TOTAL	$3,605,602.45

Note: The net value of the contributed services of the Mythical Sisters to Mythical College amounts to $150,000.00 which is the equivalent, at 4% of the income from an endowment fund of $3,750,000.00

sary for some institutions; but they will not be considered here. Each one of these funds appears separately on the balance sheet with a summary of its assets, liabilities, and balances carefully set forth as above.

In the annual financial report prepared by the auditor each fund group is supported by a subsidiary statement which gives a more detailed analysis of fund transactions and identifies the individual funds which have been grouped. The "receipts" and "disbursements" of a college which, as explained below, are *excluded* from statements of current income and current expenditures because they are designated for uses other than the current operations of the college, are to be found in these supporting statements. These receipts and disbursements are also reflected on the Condensed Balance Sheet. For that reason a discussion of each of these fund groups is given in APPENDIX VI, pages 218 through 223.

In order to give a complete financial picture of a college the balance sheet must show all of its assets and liabilities, and give the total value of the plant, the amount of indebtedness, and the principal or balances of designated funds (that is, Loan Funds, Endowment Funds, and Plant Funds).[2] The balance sheet also reflects the current position of the institution through the Current Funds Balance figure. It is to be regretted, therefore, that the published financial statements of some Catholic colleges omit the balance sheet and give only summary statements of current income and expenditures. This is only a partial financial report. A sample balance sheet for Mythical College is presented here by way of illustration. The supporting statements for the various fund groups will be found in APPENDIX VI.

Summary of Current Income

The Summary of Current Income is a record by source of all income received which is applicable to the *current operations* of the college in the year reported on. It is a condensed version of what appears in the annual auditor's report. In college accounting a distinction is made between "current income" and "receipts." Receipts (monies and the equivalents) which are to be added to the loan funds, the endowment funds, or the plant funds are *excluded* from current income, and are reported in statements of the transactions of the appropriate funds, as described in APPENDIX VI.

---

[2] *Plant valuation.* It is inadvisable to reduce plant valuation by depreciation unless a comparable cash reserve has been set up. *Appreciation* of plant valuation is quite another matter. If the market value of land is notably above the book value and there is no tax problem involved, it might be well to consider an increase in land value. Similarly, if the replacement value of buildings is considerably above the book value, it may be of advantage to revise the book values accordingly. Of course this can be done only on the testimony of reputable outside appraisal.

SUMMARY OF CURRENT INCOME
For the fiscal year ending 30 June, 1964

EDUCATIONAL AND GENERAL
Student Income

Tuition	$180,000.00	
Fees (educational)	19,500.00	
Total Student Tuition and Fees	$199,500.00	

Gifts and Grants
Restricted Income:

Endowment Income	$ 1,500.00	
Donations for restricted purposes	2,369.10	
Dividends and Interest	680.30	
Total	$ 4,549.40	

Unrestricted Income:

Foundation of Independent Colleges[3]	$ 15,690.11	
Annual Alumnae Fund	11,560.00	
Donation from Motherhouse	30,000.00	
Unrestricted Endowment Income	3,000.00	
Other gifts and donations	3,500.59	
Total	$ 63,750.70	
Contributed Services (net)[4]	$150,000.00	
Other Income	4,698.72	
Total Educational and General		$422,498.82

AUXILIARY ENTERPRISES

Dining Hall	$106,450.00	
Residence Halls	26,800.00	
Campus Store	12,100.00	
Student Activity Fees (non-educational)	4,500.00	
Total Auxiliary Enterprises		$149,850.00

STUDENT AID
Scholarships

Gifts	$ 6,980.00	
Income, Scholarship Funds	1,850.00	
Total Student Aid		$ 8,830.00
TOTAL CURRENT INCOME		$581,178.82

Current income is customarily divided into *Educational and General, Auxiliary Enterprises,* and *Student Aid.* Each main head-

---

[3] In most states the privately supported colleges of liberal arts and sciences have joined together in state-wide associations for the purpose of jointly soliciting funds from business and industry for the operating budgets of the member colleges.

[4] For an explanation of what is meant by the *net* value of contributed services refer to page 146 of the preceding chapter.

ing has various subheadings which need not be given in the summary statement with as great detail as in the annual financial report. Since we hear a great deal about the fact that student tuition and other educational fees hardly begin to pay for the cost of educating the students, it is important to distinguish the income derived from students so that anybody who wishes may readily compare it with the total Education and General Expenditures. A sample *Summary of Current Income* will be more meaningful than lengthy description.

SUMMARY OF CURRENT EXPENDITURES

The *Summary of Current Expenditures* is a record by function of all expenditures for the current operations of the college in the year reported on. Like the Summary of Current Income, it is a condensed version of what appears in greater detail in the full report. Disbursements and other charges against the principal and balances of endowment funds, loan funds, and plant funds are *excluded* from current expenditures and are reported in statements of the transactions of the appropriate funds, as described on pages 218 to 223.

The main headings are the same as on the income statement, but the subheadings will differ, especially under *Educational and General.* Here the chief subheadings are: *General Administration,* which includes the administrative offices with salaries of personnel, supplies and expenses, printing, postage and so on; *General Institutional,* which includes telephone, interest charges, insurance, membership dues, commencement, concerts, lectures and the like. *Instructional* covers anything that has to do with the teaching of students, such as salaries of teachers, supplies and expenses connected with the classroom, and so on. Under *Auxiliary Enterprises* each item should include its share of expense for plant operation and maintenance. In some cases it is appropriate to distribute a portion of general administration to auxiliaries. A sample Summary Statement of Expenditures follows:

SUMMARY OF CURRENT EXPENDITURES
For the fiscal year ending 30 June, 1964

EDUCATIONAL AND GENERAL

General Administration	$ 22,690.50	
General Institutional	65,420.50	
Instructional	260,600.30	
Library	18,300.40	
Operation of Plant	68,000.00	
Total Educational and General		$435,011.70

AUXILIARY ENTERPRISES

Dining Hall	$ 95,320.16	
Residence Halls	20,600.00	
Campus Store	8,500.32	
Student Activities (non-educational)	6,300.50	
Total Auxiliary Enterprises		$130,720.98

STUDENT AID

Scholarships	$ 8,200.00	
Grants-in-Aid	4,365.00	
Total Student Aid		$ 12,565.00
TOTAL CURRENT EXPENDITURES		$578,297.68

Needless to say no significance should be attached to the actual figures given in these sample statements. Although the figures may not be greatly out-of-line for a college of three hundred students with two-thirds of them residing on the campus, the statements are intended only to illustrate method and form.

A COMPARATIVE ANALYSIS

In order that financial statements may be more meaningful, especially for those who do not like to read figures or find financial reports confusing, some interesting facts may be pulled out from the income and expenditure statements.

For example, during the fiscal year which closed on 30 June 1964, it cost Mythical College $435,011.70 to operate its educational program. Of this amount students paid only $199,500.00 in tuition and educational fees, or about 46 percent of the cost. Thus, with an enrollment of three hundred students the educational cost to the college is $1,450.00[5] per student whereas the

---

[5] If an allowance of $32,600.50 is made for depreciation of educational buildings and equipment, the per student cost would amount to $1,558.70.

income per student is $665.00. This left a deficit on *Educational and General* account of $235,511.70 to which must be added a *Student Aid* deficit of $3,735.00. To meet this combined deficit the Mythical Sisters supplied $180,000.00, $150,000.00 in the form of contributed services and $30,000.00 in the form of an outright donation from the motherhouse. The remainder of the deficit was made up by a grant of $15,690.11 from the Foundation of Independent Colleges, by the net income of the *Auxiliary Enterprises* of $19,129.02, by the proceeds of the Annual Alumnae Fund, and by various other donations and miscellaneous income. This left a final balance of $2,881.14 as the excess of total income over total expenses for the year. The following figures tell the story.

College Educational Expenses		$435,011.70
College Income—Tuition and Educational Fees		199,500.00
Educational Deficit		235,511.70
Student Aid Deficit		3,735.00
Total Educational Deficit		$239,246.70
This Deficit was satisfied by:		
Mythical Sisters, Contributed Services	$150,000.00	
Mythical Sisters, Donation from Motherhouse	30,000.00	
Auxiliary Enterprises, Net Income	19,129.02	
Foundation of Independent Colleges	15,690.11	
Annual Alumnae Fund	11,560.00	
Other Gifts, Miscellaneous Income	15,748.71	
Total		$242,127.84
Excess of Income over Expenses		$ 2,881.14

GRAPHIC PRESENTATION

SOURCES OF THE EDUCATIONAL DOLLAR:

The Students	$	.47
From the Religious Community		.426
Annual Alumnae Fund		.028
Foundation of Independent Colleges		.038
Miscellaneous Gifts and Income		.038
	$	1.00

HOW THE EDUCATIONAL DOLLAR IS SPENT:

Instruction	$	.60
Library		.042
Administration		.052
General Expenses		.15
Operation of Plant		.156
	$	1.00

These figures, of course, lend themselves to visual representation.

WHY PUBLISH A FINANCIAL STATEMENT

It is commonly accepted today that no college worthy of the name can operate only on what is received from students in tuition and fees. Furthermore, even the substantial increases in tuition and fees have not solved the problem. Even further raises will not pay the full cost of education, which is advancing more rapidly than tuition. Besides, there is a limit beyond which tuition charges will price students out of college.

Fortunately business, industry, government, and the general public are well acquainted with this situation because of the excellent public relations efforts of various public-spirited organizations. Thus, when industrial and business concerns and foundations award scholarship grants to students, they also often make supplementary grants to the colleges which these students elect to attend, in order to make up for the gap between tuition charges and the cost of education.

Until recently Religious Communities have as a rule made no consistent and regular efforts at fund raising. Experience has proved that the money to help is available for the college that will make the necessary effort to win such support. Part of the basis for such an appeal is the willingness of a college to put its financial cards on the table. A financial statement is necessary in appeals for annual alumni funds and parents' funds, in seeking gifts and grants from friends and benefactors, from business, industry and foundations. Meanwhile many a Catholic college is paying heavily for the financial secrecy which it has maintained for so long.

With the publishing of financial reports by most of our Catholic colleges, it may be hoped that the hoary old myths of wealth that have enveloped these colleges for many years will be dispersed for good. It will then be realized that Religious Communities are not so wealthy as they have been reputed to be, and that their colleges have financial needs similar to those of other colleges.

CHAPTER 17

Development Programs

HIGHER EDUCATION is today the object of greater concern than ever before on the part of all segments of the general public. One evidence of this is the favorable climate of opinion towards voluntary donations to colleges and universities, whether privately or publicly controlled. This is the result of a combination of circumstances—some fortuitous, others promoted directly by human agencies. Although we need not explore at length the reasons for this, some reference to the factors involved will be helpful. We are concerned in this chapter with this unprecedented climate of opinion chiefly as it applies to privately supported colleges.

Paradoxically enough, World War II, which in its beginning threatened the closing of many privately supported colleges, at its ending gave the initial impetus to the rapid expansion of these colleges. The mass federal scholarships for returning military personnel not only filled the colleges, but also created a shortage of facilities. This was met in part by the Federal Government, which provided many surplus buildings and much equipment for transfer to college campuses.

Even with the decline in the number of GI students, there was no let-up in the need for additional and permanent facilities for higher education. Population growth, the rapidly rising percentage of high school graduates seeking admission to college, the general conviction that a college education is necessary to keep up with the unparalleled scientific advances in a highly mechanized society—all these have conspired to create an ever-increasing demand for higher education.

GOOD PUBLIC RELATIONS

Expert public relations activities have dramatized this situation.[1] The general public has been alerted to the needs of higher education. The various segments of the public have been convinced of their respective obligations for the support of higher education. As a consequence, federal and state legislators and agencies are now making available to colleges and universities many millions of dollars a year through loans, grants, and various contractual relations. We can add to this millions of dollars in direct governmental aid to students through loans, grants, and scholarships.

Voluntary donations from private sources have also increased by leaps and bounds. Annual alumni contributions to colleges have already passed the $220,000,000 mark. By 1964 it was estimated that annual contributions to colleges and universities by business and industrial corporations was somewhere around $225,000,000. It is hoped that this amount will more than double by 1970. Add to this, foundation gifts, individual donors among the wealthy and not so wealthy, the parents of students who contribute over and above the substantial amounts charged for education, and you have some idea of the ferment that is at work. In 1964 this annual gift support of colleges and universities climbed above the one billion dollar mark. By 1970 it is hoped that voluntary contributions from all sources will have reached an annual total of almost two billion dollars.

[1] The writer feels that a great share of the credit for the present favorable climate of opinion is due to the Council for Financial Aid to Education, Inc., the American Alumni Council, the American College Public Relations Association, and the various groups and agencies that have co-operated with them, such as the Advertising Council, the N. W. Ayer Company, and others.

All Colleges Can Benefit

This is not a largess, however, which comes to colleges and universities unsolicited. They must work for it, and work for it in a way that is purposeful, systematic, and well-co-ordinated. All the evidence indicates that every college, no matter how small, no matter where situated, and no matter under what auspices it may be conducted, can successfully obtain needed support, if it is doing a good educational job and if it will get organized properly and go to work. But only institutions that are alert, that are willing to profit by the experience of others and pay the price of efficient organization, will succeed in obtaining a proper share of the available support. This kind of organized activity is usually carried on under the name "Development Program."

Procedure for a Catholic College

Granting that there is a favorable climate for voluntary giving, how does a Catholic college go about participating in the resulting boon? Are there problems in organizing for fund raising in a Catholic college that differ significantly from those of other colleges? In general, a Catholic college must go about the job of fund raising by following the pattern that other colleges have found successful. Only up to a point will it happen that the job of organizing for fund raising in a Catholic college may differ from that of other colleges. These differences, though important, are chiefly of an organizational nature peculiar to a Catholic college, and must be set in order before a college embarks on a full-fledged development program. These are largely the problems which have been discussed in this book.

Thus a Catholic college should have its own legal charter and its own board of trustees. It should have a president who has authority and responsibility similar to that of the presidents of non-Catholic colleges. Furthermore it should have a president who is not also burdened with responsibility as superior of the Religious Community. Finally, the fiscal policies and accounting procedures of the college should be examined to see if it is separated completely from the finances of the Religious Community, both local and regional. If this has not been accomplished, it will not be possible for the college to publish financial reports and statements that are comparable to those of other colleges and universities. All of these matters have been considered in previous chapters and need not be dealt with here, except to emphasize that they are problems which affect development programs. If any of these deficiencies exist, the college must remedy them before undertaking a development program.

In addition, a Catholic college, like every other college, must first set its own house in order as an important part of the task of organizing a development program. It must give careful thought to its stated objectives and examine the kind of educational job that it is doing and wants to do. This involves at least a thorough "self-study," of the kind that the regional associations are now requiring for accrediting purposes.

LONG-RANGE PLANNING

A college must also determine precisely where it wants to go and what are to be, not only its short-term objectives—which a self-study should reveal—but also, and more especially, its long-term objectives. Where does the college want to be five, ten, or twenty years from now? Should it hold to its objectives as presently stated? What is to be the maximum enrollment for which it should plan? If there is to be an increase over the present enrollment, what should this figure be? What is the target date for reaching this figure and what yearly increments are to be planned for? What additional facilities in buildings and equipment will be required? What additional faculty will be needed? How are the necessary funds to be provided? How much must come from student tuition and fees, and how much from other specific sources.

This is called "long-range" planning. It will require at least the projection of a ten-year budget for the college and a clear statement of the various assumptions on which this is based. Long-range planning for a Catholic college also involves ways and means of finding additional Religious and clerical members for the faculty. In the first place, there must be a definite policy on the selection of suitable Religious or diocesan clergy for graduate study in the various fields of learning in which courses are offered at the college. Then there must be a definite plan to enable these selected persons to have the time off to do their graduate work at the best training schools in their respective fields. It is no easy thing for a Religious Community or a diocese to adopt an imaginative program of this kind and stick to it, when there are impossible manpower demands from every side.

This long-range planning seems to be particularly difficult for many Catholic colleges. Just why this should be so may not be immediately apparent. Paradoxical as it may seem, the same dependence on the Religious Community which was important for the foundation, growth, and the development of the college, can also stand in its way when it comes to long-range planning. Young people can be over-protected in their youth and as a consequence come to maturity with an excessive dependence on parents. In like manner, a college conducted by a Religious Community can, in a sense, be excessively dependent on the motherhouse of the Religious Community long after the necessity for this protection has ceased. There are some built-in hindrances here which can be eliminated. That is why the author insists that a college should be legally and financially separated from the motherhouse, as soon as this is possible. It should have its own charter and its own board of trustees, and there should be complete financial separation. In the absence of these requirements it is not surprising that a college finds it difficult to project a realistic ten-year budget.

When the board of trustees for the motherhouse corporation is also the board of trustees for the college, there may be many more pressing problems to face than a ten-year budget for the college. There may be immediate expansion problems to meet; a novitiate and a new juniorate to take care of the increased number of candidates for the Community; a rest home and infirmary for superannuated members; maybe a new academy in a neighboring diocese; even a new motherhouse to replace the present inadequate and unsafe building that has served for so many years. Confronted with these needs, it is no wonder that a ten-year budget for the college and possible plans for a multi-million dollar expansion program seem to be too much!

This certainly would have been too much fifteen years ago. All of these projects would have been pretty much the sole responsibility of the Religious Community, and therefore of the motherhouse corporation. Even today, with the notable exception of the college, all of these projects are still the sole responsibility of the motherhouse. But a college should be responsible for its own financing and development, and this would seem to be definitely to the advantage of the Religious Community. In order to accomplish this, it is certainly worth while clearing the way in every Catholic college and providing whatever is required for the kind of development program that is being operated successfully in hundreds of other colleges.

ORGANIZING A DEVELOPMENT PROGRAM

With the college house set reasonably in order, the procedure to be followed by a Catholic college in organizing and setting in motion a development and fund-raising program does not differ essentially from that of other comparable colleges. Although a development program has come to designate a whole new area of college and university administration, it embraces at least three basic activities that are not new in themselves: alumni and alumnae affairs, public relations and publicity; and fund raising of every type. It is the coordination of these activities and the new techniques which are comparatively recent. The coordination of these activities in one area of administration should not interfere with any essential autonomy of either the alumni office or the public relations office.

The alumni situation in many Catholic colleges presents a problem in the organization of a modern development program. Alumni groups in these colleges are wary of giving up any measure of independence in the interest of better integration with the college and its development program. In the past, the administrators of Catholic colleges have encouraged alumni organizations to be independent of the college, chiefly to get them to be self-supporting and thus to relieve the college of the burden of support. In some instances this encouragement has gone as far as separate incorporation for the alumni organization. Now, paradoxically, the trend is reversed. The modern way is for the alumni office to be an integral part of the administrative setup of the college. The college no longer worries about the expenses of the alumni office, because they have been absorbed into the regular college budget. The custom of "annual alumni giving," with no strings attached, more than makes up for the outlay.

The proper integration of the alumni setup into the whole development program of the college is of the utmost importance. Where it does not exist, it behooves the college president to bring it about as tactfully and expeditiously as possible. He should be humbly conscious of past history in the attitude of the college administration, and then patiently set about bringing the alumni situation into line. This is a matter for his personal attention in dealing with alumni officers and leaders, to convince them that the giving up of a little seeming independence will redound to the benefit of both the college and the alumni organization. Furthermore, these benefits should be clearly pointed out. A president can also allude to the fact that this is now modern alumni thinking and practice in most colleges and universities.

DIRECTOR OF DEVELOPMENT

This new area of college administration requires an administrator who has the imagination and the ability to get a development program off the ground and keep it moving. The question is often asked who should be chosen to head the development program of a Catholic college, especially a Catholic college for women. There is, of course, no pat answer. Successful directors of development programs in women's colleges may be Religious, laywomen, or laymen. There is likewise no set pattern for Catholic men's colleges or coeducational colleges. The main thing is to select one who has the intelligence, the competence and the experience— or at least the willingness and the ability to gain the necessary experience without loss of time.

Several different titles have been given to this official. *Director of Development* is the most expressive if not the most common. Some institutions have designated this administrator as "Vice President for Development." This is presumed to give the person in charge of development greater prestige both within and without the institution. But there are valid objections to this in a college of moderate enrollment. Vice president means literally one who takes the place of the president whenever the need arises. If there is to be a vice president in charge of development, a lopsided situation is created if the academic dean, who is normally thought of as second in command to the president, is not also a vice president. The term is wrenched from its accepted meaning when it is given as a title to one who is not and cannot be second in command, or when there are two or more vice presidents—especially in a college of moderate size. In multiplying vice presidents to give added importance to individuals, a college runs the risk of sacrificing the ready communication and unity of effort which are required for effective operation. Any situation which involves too many chiefs and not enough Indians is usually self-defeating. The title "Assistant to the President" or "Assistant to the President for Development" would seem to be more appropriate.

But far more important than the title, for a layman who may be chosen to head the development program, is the fact that he must be taken completely into the college and must have the full confidence of administration and faculty. He must be truly involved in all the inner counsels of the college. He must be fully informed of all its hopes, plans, problems, and vicissitudes. To this end he should sit in on the meetings and discussions of all top-level boards and committees. This does not mean that he should necessarily take an active part in these meetings. He is there chiefly to observe and understand, and to respond to such questions as may be directed to him. He must studiously avoid trying to dictate policy on matters that are not his immediate responsibility. He should not expect the purchasing department, for example, to buy products only from companies which contribute funds to the college, regardless of other considerations.

A director of development must be given adequate assistance. In the beginning secretarial assistance may be sufficient. But once things begin to get organized there will have to be competent assistants in public relations or fund raising, as circumstances may require. It is important to have a proper office set-up in a prominent place on the campus, with adjoining space for the component activities of alumni, public relations, and fund raising. An adequate budget is of course essential. No fixed amount can be recommended. Those with experience estimate that it costs at least ten to fifteen cents for each dollar raised. Presumably the cost will be much higher until a program is well established. One must be prepared for the fact that it costs money to raise voluntary gift money.

A development program is expensive. It may take two, three, or even more years before the program begins to pay its way. Occasionally one encounters religious administrators who expect that once they have engaged a director of development and have committed themselves to a sizable salary, he should be able single-handed to obtain gifts from individuals and foundations which will offset what the college has already invested in the program. They expect that at least this ought to be done before additional assistants can be engaged, and before there can be an increase in the budget for the development office.

Much depends on how well the college is organized internally, what kind of public relations program it has been carrying on, what kind of news or information bureau has been functioning, how well the alumni are organized and how well prepared they are to accept integration into a full-scale development program. How well organized are the friends of the college? What has been done to build up lists of prospective givers? These are all important preparatory steps. The college that is starting out on a development program is bound to be sadly disillusioned, if it thinks that there is any short cut to substantial fund raising. It would be a mistake to think that all problems are solved once a competent, high salaried director has been engaged.

Finally, there must be a realistic order of priority. Those tasks which are closest at hand must be tackled first—annual alumni donations and parents' fund efforts, for example. Then there are the activities in which trustees and members of the associate board must help, such as solicitation from business and industrial corporations. There are also the longer-range programs which deal with special gifts, wills, bequests and the like. These require careful preparation and patient cultivation on the part of many selected individuals, and ought not be attempted until the development office is well established.

INVOLVE EVERYONE

Practically speaking, the president of the college will have to be the sparkplug, both in getting the program started and in keeping it going. His close association with the program is inescapable. No matter how able and efficient his development staff may be, the president must be able and willing to give time to it generously. But to succeed, a development program must involve everyone connected with the college. The members of the board of trustees, who have a particular responsibility for raising funds for operational and capital purposes, have special reason to be interested. They must not only show initiative in setting up the program and establishing the immediate and long-range goals, but must also approve the budget and appoint or authorize a director. They must not only help to get the program off the ground but also keep it moving by their enthusiasm.

Next to the board of trustees, the associate board, which is organized to cooperate closely with the trustees, has a primary stake in the development program and should be in on all planning from the beginning. This board should be picked with the development program in mind, because much of the high level work will depend on its members.

Faculty members must also be involved, especially in the planning aspects of the program. They ought to be able to propound a clear statement of objectives and to recommend decisions as to where the college ought to be five, ten, or twenty years in the future. An enrollment goal must be set, a statement of realistic needs must be prepared and spelled out with reasons set forth. Finally, there must be agreement as to the priorities to be observed in the fulfillment of needs.

In brief, the administrative officers, the faculty, the non-academic staff and the alumni must all be involved. Every practicable means must be used to arouse their interest and to enlist their whole-hearted and continuing support. In fact, no one who has any part, be it ever so humble and obscure, in the operation of the college can be overlooked.

TIME IS SHORT

The author has made no attempt to deal with development programs exhaustively. For the most part he has limited himself to highlighting difficulties which some Catholic colleges experience in organizing development programs. For the reader interested in greater detail there is an abundance of literature available in this whole area.[2] There is need perhaps for only one further comment here.

For those colleges which have been debating the wisdom of a development program, let it be said that time is running out. A continuous program of fund raising has long since passed the experimental stage. Results in the case of many colleges which have undertaken development programs are regularly published for all to read. Moreover, those who have the know-how are apparently eager to share their knowledge and experience with other colleges. What reason can there be for further delay? The case has been summed up succinctly, if not completely, by one educator:

> Institutions which lag behind in their long-range planning efforts will soon find themselves out-distanced by competing colleges and universities which have developed more appealing programs to attract high quality students and financial support.

[2] See "Selected Bibliography on College Relations and Development," Washington, D.C., American College Public Relations Associations, Revised Edition, 1965. See also Jones/Stanford/White, *Letters to College Presidents* (Englewood Cliffs, New Jersey: Prentice-Hall, Inc., 1964), especially Chapters XIX, XX, XXI and XXII.

CHAPTER 18

Interinstitutional Cooperation

ONE OF the urgent trends today in higher education in the United States is "interinstitutional cooperation." The name is comparatively new, but not the reality it represents—at least not in the experience of a minority of institutions of higher education. Interinstitutional cooperation is based on the fact that no one college or university by itself has the requisite staff, equipment, facilities and money to do all the things it would like to do for its students, especially in important areas that appeal to small numbers of students. When two or more colleges join together to share their resources, it is possible to do for students what could not be done by a single institution.

Paradoxically enough it was the wealthier institutions, the ones which seemed to have least need of collaboration, which first made use of interinstitutional cooperation and have been carrying it on successfully for many years. But the less wealthy colleges, the colleges which seemed to have most to gain by joining forces and working together, have persisted in their isolation until economic forces have begun to threaten their very existence.

Catholic colleges have probably delayed longer than other colleges in considering the possibilities of interinstitutional cooperation. Not only have they failed to cooperate academically with other colleges; they have failed to cooperate among themselves in academic matters, although presumably as a group they have

174

more in common than other colleges. Fortunately there is tangible evidence that Catholic colleges have awakened to the need of collaborating with other colleges and now realize the benefits attainable by pooling resources in some form or other.

THREE CURRENT PROBLEMS

The absence of any academic collaboration or joint planning among Catholic colleges in the past has spawned a needless and dangerous proliferation of new, small and unavoidably weak colleges. This has led to three situations, more or less distinct, which now demand thought and attention. Unless the tendencies involved can be controlled by collaboration, many of the small institutions are headed for failure. First is the proliferation of colleges intended exclusively for the education of Religious. Second is the proliferation of colleges for lay students which in many instances may be motivated by an underlying desire to provide educational opportunities for specific Religious Communities. Finally, there is the situation of the existing Catholic colleges, especially those established in the past ten or fifteen years, for which, in many instances, the future is very doubtful.

COLLEGES FOR SISTERS

The evidence of proliferation of new Catholic colleges for Sisters is rather startling. An NCEA Research Office report reveals that there are now 93 colleges for the education of Sisters, 49 of which have been founded in the ten-year period ending in 1963. At the date of the report only three of the 49 recently founded colleges were regionally accredited and only four of them enrolled 100 or more students. These colleges undoubtedly involve great cost to the Religious Communities. They tie down a relatively large number of highly qualified teachers who are badly needed elsewhere. Nevertheless, by all present-day standards, most of these colleges must be considered weak institutions, and attainment and retention of proper accreditation will be a perennial problem.

But the fact is that these Religious Communities have a real problem in providing for the education of their Sisters, who staff Catholic primary and secondary schools as well as many colleges. Their problem is twofold, to provide sound education while developing spiritual formation and religious commitment—a matter of great importance not only for the individual Religious Communities but for the whole of Catholic education. It will not suffice to condemn the mushrooming of these small, weak colleges unless alternative proposals can be presented.

Interinstitutional cooperation is a way to meet the problem and fortunately the time is ripe for it. The artificial barriers to collaboration among Religious Communities are rapidly disappearing, so that the way is now open to cooperative efforts in solving these problems. The Sister Formation Conference[1] has done much to bring the various Religious Communities together for discussion and study at both national and regional conferences. This has had a very helpful influence in promoting cooperation among the Religious Orders of women.

Well-established Catholic liberal arts colleges, and the larger colleges and universities, must all lend a hand. The small institutions open to lay students believe—and rightly so—that the number of Sister students must always be kept in a minority if the nature of the institution is not to change. Because of their dress, their religious consecration, and their apostolic commitment, Sisters constitute an unmistakably unique element in a student community. The larger colleges and universities are in a better position to share their resources with these Religious Communities, in such a way that their legitimate religious aims are not jeopardized while they strive for excellence in academic achievement.

There are many ways through which collaboration between Religious Communities can be carried out. Patterns of cooperation for both large and small institutions are now to be found in the ever-increasing instances of collaboration. Among methods thus far employed we mention: arrangements whereby Religious

---

[1] The Sister Formation is a national movement with a permanent Secretariat in Washington, D.C. through which the various Religious Communities of women have cooperated in setting more exacting standards and developing more effective procedures for the higher education, spiritual, cultural, and professional development of young Sisters before they undertake their mission as teachers.

Communities supply their own residence accommodations, but make use of the academic facilities of an existing college and contribute a quota of qualified faculty members to its faculty; a college institution for Sisters only, in which several Religious Communities participate; the establishment by an existing college of off-campus centers for other Religious Communities that are reasonably close by. In mentioning the selected examples of cooperation which follow we make no claim to being exhaustive; we merely wish to illustrate a variety of cooperative projects.

Alverno College in Milwaukee is a well-established, fully accredited liberal arts college for women with excellent plant facilities and equipment. With an enrollment of about 1000 lay students, it is now serving as the collegiate center for Sisters of all provinces of the School Sisters of St. Francis, who operate the college. It also serves as the collegiate center for Sisters of three independent Religious Communities from North Dakota, Indiana, and Pennsylvania respectively. Each Community provides its own study house on or adjacent to the Alverno campus. Teaching positions on the Alverno faculty are available to qualified Sisters of these Communities.

A somewhat similar cooperative arrangement for men is to be found at *Saint Mary's College,* at Winona, Minnesota. Here a well-established, fully accredited liberal arts college for men, operated by the Christian Brothers, now serves as the collegiate center for a scholasticate of the Christian Brothers, for the collegiate seminary of the diocese of Winona, and for the collegiate seminary of the Sacred Heart Fathers, all of which have their own separate residences on the campus but whose students attend the regular college classes.

Rosary College at River Forest, Illinois, a fully accredited liberal arts college conducted by Dominican Sisters and enrolling about 1000 lay students, has been serving for several years as the collegiate center for the Sisters of Saint Joseph of LaGrange, Illinois. A number of Saint Joseph Sisters teach regularly on the faculty.

Marillac College, Normandy, Missouri, is a cooperative venture in which several Religious Communities participate. It is an accredited liberal arts college exclusively for Sisters. The participating Communities establish adjacent houses of study. Doctorate-level faculty members are drawn from the various participating Communities.

In Washington, D.C., across the street from the *Trinity College* campus, six different Religious Communities of Sisters are co-operating in the establishment of an educational center for Sisters. It is to be affiliated with Trinity College, and will also permit students to take advantage of courses in the ten colleges and universities in the Washington area.

De Mattias Hall at *Saint Louis University* is a residence hall for Sisters owned and operated by a Community of Sisters from Illinois. These Sisters have a cooperative collegiate arrangement with Saint Louis University. They built this center primarily for their own Sisters, but also for other Sisters attending Saint Louis University, whether at the graduate or the undergraduate level.

The University of Dallas, a coeducational institution operated under the auspices of the Diocese of Dallas-Fort Worth, has an extensive new campus overlooking the city of Dallas, Texas. The president and the academic dean of this institution are laymen, but the faculty is made up of Religious and diocesan priests, Sisters, and laymen and laywomen. This institution is willing and able to supply campus sites for Religious Communities to build their own study houses, with the understanding that each Community will supply a certain quota of qualified faculty members. Thus far, the Sisters of St. Mary and the Cistercian Fathers have built study houses, and members of these Communities serve on the university faculty. Dominican Fathers, who serve as chaplains and as faculty members, have also built a residence on the campus.

There are a number of instances in which an accredited college, operated by one Religious Community, assists in the academic preparation of Sisters of another Community. This is done through a cooperative arrangement which includes the establishment of an approved branch campus-center for the first two years of college work. In such cases it is of great importance that the educational program and faculty of the branch campus be under the direct control and administrative supervision of the sponsoring college, so that there can be no question as to equivalency of the academic program and no danger to the accredited status of the mother institution.

Colleges for Lay Students

In addition to the proliferation of colleges intended exclusively for the education of Religious, there has been an alarming proliferation of colleges for lay students. Between 1950 and 1964 at least 39 new Catholic colleges for lay students were established, 28 four-year colleges and 11 junior colleges. It is difficult to find a reasonable justification for most of these colleges. Some of them, although classified as colleges for lay students, have undoubtedly been undertaken primarily to provide education for the Sisters of the Religious Community, while lay students have been included in the belief that this will lessen the financial burden on the Community. If history repeats itself, many of the colleges now designated exclusively for Religious will eventually expand to include lay students.

There is a plausible argument that Catholic day colleges are needed in some areas where young people cannot afford to go away to college because of the expenses of board, room, and travel. But in most cases it does not seem to work out that way. The young people for whom the college was presumably founded take the tuition which they can afford to pay to the local college, seek scholarship help and part-time work, borrow the rest of the money from the government, and go off to a college away from home because they prefer it. In other instances a new publicly supported college moves in next door to a Catholic day college and takes over the local clientele. The result has been that the local Catholic college has had to seek funds to build residence halls in order to stay alive.

In a few instances new colleges have been established in areas where there is no Catholic college within a 100-mile radius. But this is the rare exception, not the rule. For example, in 1950 there were thirteen states which did not have even one Catholic senior college. In the following fourteen years only two of the 28 new four-year Catholic colleges were established in these states, and only three other colleges were opened in areas reasonably distant from existing Catholic colleges. For the most part these colleges have been established in areas which were already supplied with Catholic colleges. In some instances new colleges have been established within easy walking distance of an existing Catholic college which caters to the same clientele. It is difficult to avoid the impression that these colleges have been founded to meet the desires and ambitions of Religious Communities rather than the convenience and need of the Catholic population.

The alarming proliferation of new Catholic colleges, at a time when the cost of operating colleges has skyrocketed, is not only a perilous financial adventure but a substantial threat to the survival of *all* Catholic colleges of liberal arts. The initial investment in land and buildings is only a beginning. No matter how well established a college may be, it never seems to be finished with the job of replacing outmoded facilities or providing new facilities and raising the funds necessary to pay for them. Most of this money must come from Catholic sources. Unless Religious Communities and others responsible for the establishment of Catholic institutions of higher education are guided by a carefully developed plan to meet the critical needs of the Catholic population of this country, with optimum use of the limited resources of manpower and facilities, the appeal to Catholic philanthropists and others for funds is doomed to failure.

CURRENT EXAMPLES OF COOPERATION

Although the problems of providing for proper Sister formation and avoiding the proliferation of both Religious and lay colleges are undoubtedly matters of great importance, there is also the serious problem of what to do with the many existing Catholic colleges of liberal arts, how to strengthen them and how to insure survival. All of these problems are closely intertwined, and the only promise of solution is through interinstitutional cooperation.

From what has already been said it should be evident that interinstitutional cooperation is now a reality for some Catholic colleges. But there is still a long way to go. Catholic institutions have been slow to see the need and the possibilities of collaborating with other colleges and universities, both Catholic and non-

Catholic. The prevailing tendency has been to compete rather than to collaborate. Only recently have Catholic colleges begun even to consider collaboration with other institutions. Voluntary cooperation will better serve the common cause than competition and isolation, for in this way the whole of higher education will be stronger than through the mere accumulation of isolated institutions. There is much to learn from the experience of other colleges in developing methods of doing this.

Cooperation among existing colleges has already taken many forms which involve the pooling of resources for graduate studies and permit a free interchange of students and professors. On the undergraduate level there are also many forms, involving the joint use of libraries, science laboratories, and other facilities. Some groups of colleges have agreed to delimit certain specialized fields in which each will develop, making courses and faculty members available to the students from the cooperating institutions. Library resources have been pooled by merging library catalogues so that joint library facilities will be available to all students in the cooperating colleges. Teachers in certain fields for which there may not be great student demand have been shared, and classes of two or more institutions have been merged in courses where enrollments tend to be small. Even the joint engagement of professional talent for instruction has been put into use.

In giving illustrations of these various forms of cooperation in which Catholic institutions participate, one runs the risk of neglecting to mention even more significant examples. But it is worth while taking that risk to make it clear that there is no set pattern for interinstitutional cooperation. There are almost as many possibilities as there are colleges or groups of colleges.

A very interesting project of interinstitutional cooperation has been undertaken in Washington, D.C. The five universities in the District of Columbia—American, Catholic, Georgetown, George Washington and Howard—in 1964 formed the "Joint Graduate Consortium of Washington Universities" by agreeing to pool their facilities for graduate study under one director. Under this arrangement a graduate student enrolled at any one of the five universities is able to take one or more courses at any of the others. The degree will be awarded by the university in which the student originally enrolled. A similar agreement in the field of graduate nursing has been entered into by Washington and Saint Louis Universities with the intention of extending it to other graduate programs.

One of the earliest projects of interinstitutional cooperation in which Catholic colleges participated is the "Four College Area Studies," which was initiated in 1953 with the help of Louis W. and Maud Hill Family Foundation of St. Paul. Here four privately supported, church-related colleges, two Catholic and two Protestant, have been carrying on an integrated area study program for undergraduates offered by the faculties of the four colleges. No one of the colleges—Hamline University, Macalester College, the College of St. Catherine, and the College of St. Thomas—would have been able singly to offer its students the advantages of these courses because of the enrollment, staff, and financial problems involved. A somewhat similar program was undertaken in 1962 by six small colleges located within a 35-mile radius in Pennsylvania and Maryland, namely, Dickinson and Gettysburg colleges in Pennsylvania and Hood, Mount St. Mary's, St. Joseph and Western Maryland colleges in Maryland. A grant from the Ford Foundation assisted the program.[2]

In Rochester, New York, Nazareth College and St. John Fisher College have combined their library catalogues so that the facilities of both institutions are available to the students of both colleges. Furthermore, young women of Nazareth College majoring in science take their upper division courses at St. John Fisher, while the young men of this latter college take their art and music courses at Nazareth. A similar arrangement is in effect between Mount St. Vincent and Manhattan Colleges in New York.

Saint Louis University, Fontbonne, and Webster Colleges—all in the St. Louis area, have agreed to delimit certain specialized fields so that one institution can develop exclusively in that field with the purpose of serving all three institutions. Thus it was agreed that Webster College should develop in music. With this

[2] See *Non-Western Studies in the Liberal Arts College,* Association of American Colleges, Washington, D.C., 20009, 1964.

assurance, the college lost no time in acquiring additional facilities and shortly thereafter received a million-dollar gift for its music program. Undoubtedly this program was more attractive to the donor because it would serve not one but three institutions.

In Minnesota the College of St. Benedict, St. John's University and St. Cloud State College conducted a joint program in "General Education for Faculty Members and Superior Students." This program also had foundation support.

In central Texas eleven colleges—four Catholic, five Protestant, and two state-operated—have been cooperating for a few years in a television project. They are linked in a closed-circuit network through the use of coaxial cable and microwave transmission. Programs originate at the University of Texas in Austin or at one of the commercial stations in San Antonio.

No two of these examples are exactly alike.[3] They illustrate the almost unlimited opportunities for interinstitutional cooperation among Catholic colleges, between Catholic and Protestant colleges, and between Catholic and state colleges. In every instance there have been obstacles to overcome. There are hurdles to clear in planning, adjustment and accommodations. Once a college decides to enter a cooperative program with other colleges, there must be willingness to surrender a certain amount of independence of action, a willingness to give and take in the matter of institutional self-interest. In most cases helpful collaboration is possible where there is good will, imagination, and willingness to work together. The low student-teacher ratio common in the small college can no longer be defended or claimed as an asset. It is often a waste of human teaching resources. Much wasteful duplication of courses could be eliminated and a more economical use of teachers could be fostered through the cooperative planning of two or more colleges.

Is Interinstitutional Cooperation Enough?

The head of a large non-Catholic university once mentioned to the writer a particular area in which there were seven or eight

---

[3] See *Inter-Institutional Cooperation*, National Catholic Educational Association Bulletin, Washington, D.C., 20036, February, 1964.

Catholic colleges in close proximity, most of them struggling along with comparatively small enrollments and inadequate facilities. Why, he asked, wouldn't one college or, if you wish, two colleges, one for men and one for women, be able to do a better educational job? With the combined resources and the combined enrollments of all the existing colleges, one or two colleges could provide more competent faculties, more adequate library, and other facilities; and they would do a much better educational job.

It is not easy to reply to such a question because one must admit that the questioner's assumptions are correct. In the past the writer has resorted to the very un-ecumenical statement that it would probably be easier to persuade Baptists, Lutherans and Methodists to combine in the conduct of one college than to get two or more different Religious Orders of the Catholic Church to do so. Then, if one does not wish to suggest rivalries or petty jealousies, one falls back on the explanation that each one of these Religious Orders takes pride in its own particular spirit, traditions, and independence, which it thinks would be slighted, lost, or destroyed in a college which was the merged operation of two or more different Religious Communities.

Although the merging of existing colleges may not be feasible at present, the joint operation of a college by two or more different Religious Communities does not seem to be the impossibility it was a few years ago. For many years now a number of large diocesan high schools have been conducted by the cooperative efforts of several Religious Communities working in the same high school. There is also a diocesan college in the Middle West where the clerical faculty is made up equally of priests of the diocese and priests of a Religious Community. Many of the larger Catholic universities have long had faculty members who belong to Religious Communities other than that which sponsors the college. These are all joint undertakings, but in each instance the financial responsibility and the ultimate control resides in the diocese or in a single Religious Community. The writer envisages the day when the founding of a new college will be the joint undertaking of two or more Religious Communities, which will accept a proportionate share of responsibility for the financing and operation of the college.

There are some who consider that even more radical steps are required to safeguard the interests of Catholic education as a whole. It has been suggested, for example, that some small Catholic colleges be closed or converted into junior colleges. Others believe that there should be a moratorium on new Catholic colleges until there is a national plan for Catholic colleges, a program for geographical distribution, a proved need for each college proposed, and some assurance of support. There is undoubtedly some merit in these suggestions, but a discussion of them would extend beyond the limits of this chapter.

APPENDIX I

Sample Charters

FOUR SAMPLE CHARTERS (articles of incorporation) have been selected from a collection of charters of Catholic colleges in the possession of the writer. These particular examples have been chosen because they are fairly recent, they represent different states, and they are for colleges operated by different Religious Communities. Furthermore, these charters illustrate some of the desiderata mentioned in Chapter I. For the most part they have considerable flexibility. They deal with the government and management of the college only in general terms, and avoid laying down qualifications for trustees and the like, leaving all these details to the bylaws which boards of trustees are empowered to adopt. They make no distinction between the corporation and the board of trustees. The first two do not restrict the activities of the college to either men or women and make no unnecessary limitations on curricula. However, the broad, flexible type of charter permissible in one state may not be possible in another state.

CHARTER "A"

Charter "A," from the State of Kansas, was granted in 1933 to a Catholic college for women operated by a Religious Community of women. It follows the printed form which was available for use in that state. The following items about this charter are noteworthy: (a) the corporate existence is set at fifty years, since Kansas is one of the few states which do not grant perpetual charters; (b) there is no mention that the college was founded specifically for women; (c) there is no mention of the Religious Community which founded and operates the college; (d) although the number of members of the board of directors is rigidly specified at seven, there is no limitation on their qualifications for membership; (e) there is no mention of the legal rights and privileges of the corporation, presumably because the law of Kansas provides that these are automatically included with incorporation and do not have to be specifically mentioned. The actual wording of the charter follows:

The undersigned, citizens of the State of Kansas, do hereby associate ourselves together for the purpose of forming a private corporation under the laws of the State of Kansas, and do hereby certify:

FIRST: That the name of this corporation shall be .... College.

SECOND: That this corporation is organized not for profit, and that the purposes for which it is formed are: To establish, support, and maintain a college for the promotion and encouragement of education and teaching the arts and sciences in all their various forms and the support of literary and scientific undertakings, the maintenance of a library and promotion and encouragement of painting, music and other fine arts.

THIRD: That the place where its business is to be transacted is at and near ....Kansas.

FOURTH: That the term for which this corporation is to exist is Fifty Years.

FIFTH: That the number of directors of this corporation shall be seven (7) and the names and residences of those who are appointed for the first year are:

> (Then follow the names and addresses of seven persons all of whom on the original board were Sisters of the Religious Community which sponsored the College.)

In Testimony whereof, We have hereunto subscribed our names, this 30th day of September, A.D. 1933

(Then follow the signatures of the seven incorporators, and the testimony and seal of a Notary Public.)

(Eleven days later the charter was officially filed at the Office of Secretary of State and acknowledged.)

✿   ✿   ✿

CHARTER "B"

Charter "B" is from the Commonwealth of Massachusetts and was granted in 1947 for a college intended and operated exclusively for the preparation of teachers of a Religious Community of women. Nevertheless the charter is not unnecessarily restricted or limited in any way. There is no mention of the Religious Community nor are the seven incorporators identified as Sisters, although presumably they were members of the Religious Community which sponsored the College. The wording of the charter follows:

THE COMMONWEALTH OF MASSACHUSETTS

Be it known that whereas Helen T. Smith, Janice Jones, Helen E. Black, Susan M. Brown, Janet F. Cook, Ruth F. Sullivan and Alice Maynall [1] have associated themselves with the intention of forming a corporation in accordance with the provision of Chapter 180, of the General Laws under the name of...................College.

For the purpose of the following:—To maintain and conduct a college for the teaching of the liberal arts, of the sciences and of kindred subjects with authority to grant and confer all degrees such as are usually conferred by colleges of the Commonwealth of Massachusetts except degrees in medicine and law (other than honorary doctorates):— To acquire by purchase, gift, bequest or devise, money, personal property, both tangible and intangible, and real property which may be necessary or proper to the accomplishment of the purposes hereinbefore stated; and have complied with the provisions of the Statutes of this Commonwealth in such case made and provided, as appears from the Articles of Organization of said corporation, duly approved by the Commissioner of Corporations and Taxation[2] and recorded in this office:

---

[1] Names are fictitious.
[2] This function is now performed by the Board of Collegiate Authority.

Now, therefore, I, Frederick W. Cook, Secretary of the Commonwealth of Massachusetts DO HEREBY CERTIFY that said Helen T. Smith, Janice Jones, Helen E. Black, Susan M. Brown, Janet F. Cook, Ruth F. Sullivan and Alice Maynall, their associates and successors, are legally organized and established as, and are hereby made, an existing corporation as of January 30, 1947 under the name of ....College, with the powers, rights and privileges, and subject to the limitations, duties and restrictions, which by law apertain thereto.

Witness my official signature hereunto subscribed and the Great Seal of the Commonwealth of Massachusetts hereunto affixed, this twenty-fourth day of March in the year of Our Lord one thousand nine hundred and forty-seven.

*　　*　　*

CHARTER "C"

Charter "C" was granted by the State of Virginia in 1960 to a Junior College which had been founded by a Religious Community of women and had operated previously under a charter issued in another state and "domesticated" in Virginia. The charter is broad enough for a four year college but is unnecessarily limited to women. There is no mention of the Religious Community and no restrictions as to whom may be members of the nine-man board of directors. (The original board of directors was composed of clergy, sisters and laymen.)

ARTICLES OF INCORPORATION

We, the undersigned, desiring to associate ourselves as a corporation, pursuant to Chapter 2 of Title 12 of the 1950 Code of Laws of Virginia, do certify as follows:

FIRST: The name of the corporation shall be "...................... College."

SECOND: The purposes for the formation of the corporation are as follows:

(a) The continuance of an educational institution to train young women to utilize their opportunities and advantages, through an integrated program of religious, intellectual, physical and social activity, to help themselves and all mankind.

(b) To award diplomas and degrees to students who have completed the prescribed courses.

The foregoing shall be construed both as objects and powers, and it is hereby expressly provided that the foregoing enumeration of specific powers shall not be held to limit or restrict in any manner the powers of this corporation under the general laws of this State.

THIRD: The corporation is to have no members.

FOURTH: The directors, names herein, shall continue to act as such directors until their death, resignation or removal from office, at which time a successor will be elected by a majority of the remaining directors.

FIFTH: The term for which the corporation is organized shall be perpetual.

SIXTH: The initial registered office of the corporation shall be......
.............., Virginia, and the name of the initial registered agent is........................, a resident of the State of Virginia, a director of the corporation and a member of the Bar of Virginia.

SEVENTH: The initial Board of Directors will be composed of nine (9) persons whose names and residences are as follows:

❖   ❖   ❖

Charter "D"

Some States now require specific mention in the charter of the curricula to be offered and the degrees to be confirmed. This is the case in New York where the following charter was granted in 1961 for a college conducted under the auspices of a Religious Community of women:

THE UNIVERSITY OF THE STATE OF NEW YORK
EDUCATION DEPARTMENT
ABSOLUTE CHARTER OF
......................COLLEGE

This instrument witnesseth THAT THE BOARD OF REGENTS FOR AND ON BEHALF OF THE EDUCATION DEPARTMENT OF THE STATE OF NEW YORK HAS GRANTED THIS ABSO-LUTE CHARTER.

1. Incorporating (one clergyman, two Sisters, and three laymen are named) and their associates and successors as an educational corporation under the corporate name of ....College,

to be located in the city of.............. county and State of New York.

2. The purposes for which such corporation is formed are to establish and maintain a liberal arts college for women, lay and religious, and to conduct therein courses of study leading to the degrees of bachelor of arts (B.A.) and bachelor of science (B.S.) with authority in the corporation to confer said degrees and also the honorary degrees of doctor of laws (L.L.D.), doctor of letters (Litt.D.), doctor of humane letters (L.H.D.) and doctor of fine arts (D.F.A.), in conformity with the Rules of the Regents of the University and the Regulations of the Commissioner of Education for the registration of institutions of higher education.

3. (Repeating the names given above in #1.) shall constitute the first board of trustees. The Board shall have power to adopt bylaws, including therein provisions fixing the method of election and the term of office of trustees, and shall have power also, by vote of three-fourths of all the members of the board of trustees, to change the number of trustees, to be not more than twenty-five (25) nor less than five (5).

4. The corporation hereby created shall be a nonstock corporation organized and operated exclusively for educational purposes, and no part of its earnings or net income shall inure to the benefit of any individual, and no officer, member or employee of the corporation shall receive or be entitled to receive any pecuniary profit from the operation thereof, except reasonable compensation for services.

5. The principal office of the corporation is to be located in the city of........................, ... county and State of New York.

6. The Commissioner of Education is designated as the representative of the corporation upon whom process in any action or proceeding against it may be served.

✿   ✿   ✿

Bylaws of Board of Trustees
of Mythical College

ARTICLE I—NAME

The legal name of this corporation is Mythical College, hereinafter referred to as the College. The principal office of the College is in Fictitious City, State of Jackson.

ARTICLE II—PURPOSE

The purpose of the College is to further the higher education of youths and adults and to confer such degrees upon the completion of such curricula as shall be established from time to time by the Board of Trustees and the administration and faculty of the College, in accordance with the provisions of its charter and the laws of the State of Jackson.

ARTICLE III—BOARD OF TRUSTEES [1]

Section 1. The property, affairs, business, and concerns of the College shall be vested in the Board of Trustees, subject to the provisions of law and of the Charter of the College.

Section 2. The Board of Trustees shall consist of seven members, a majority of which shall be members of the Congregation of Mythical Sisters, Jackson Province.

---

[1] Sometimes called Board of Directors, Board of Overseers, etc.

Section 3. The following shall be *ex officio* members of the Board of Trustees, the Provincial of the Jackson Province of the Congregation of Mythical Sisters, who shall serve as chairman, the Religious Superior of the religious community attached to the College, who shall serve as Vice Chairman; the President of the College who shall serve as Secretary-Treasurer. In the event that the President and the Religious Superior are one and the same person, the Provincial shall designate another Sister to serve as *ex officio* Vice Chairman and member of the Board of Trustees.

Section 4. The remaining members of the Board of Trustees, at least two of whom shall be lay persons, shall be nominated by the Chairman and elected by the *ex officio* members of the Board. Vacancies among the elected members of the Board shall be filled in like manner, through election by the remaining members of the Board.

Section 5. The term of elected members shall be three years or until their successors are duly elected. As far as possible provision shall be made for overlapping terms. A trustee may be re-elected.

ARTICLE IV—POWERS AND DUTIES

Section 1. The Board of Trustees shall bear full and complete responsibility for the College as a corporate entity. It shall formulate and determine or approve such general policies as shall be deemed necessary for the administration and development of the College.

Section 2. It shall choose a President and other principal officers as shall be needed for the operation and control of the College. All such officers shall be directly responsible to the President of the College.

Section 3. It shall exercise general supervision over the work of the administrative officers of the College, pass upon the satisfactoriness of the service rendered, and decide upon the retention or dismissal of officers.

ARTICLE V—MEETINGS

Section 1. There shall be at least four regular meetings of the Board of Trustees to be held during the months of January, March, May and October. The January meeting shall be considered the annual meeting. Due notice of all meetings shall be given by the Secretary in writing, either personally or by mail, to all members of the Board.

Section 2. Special meetings of the Board may be called by the Chairman, or in his absence or inability to act, by the Vice Chairman or Secretary.

Section 3. The presence in person or by proxy of a majority of the members of the Board of Trustees shall be necessary to constitute a quorum for the transaction of business. A majority vote of those present shall be sufficient for any decision or election.

ARTICLE VI—ASSOCIATE BOARD [2]

Section 1. The board of Trustees may choose up to twenty-five suitable lay persons as an associate board to be known as the "Board of........" (whatever title may be adopted). The members thereof shall serve individually for a term of three years and may be reappointed after an interval of one year. The President of the College and the lay members of the Board of Trustees shall be *ex officio* members of the (associate board). An executive secretary for this board shall be appointed by the President of the College from the administrative staff of the College.

Section 2. The (associate board) shall be concerned with ways and means of promoting the expansion and development of the College by increasing revenues for current operations, endowments, scholarships, building projects, and such other matters as may be referred to it from time to time by the Board of Trustees.

Section 3. Any individual member of the (associate board), without the necessity of a formal meeting of the Board, shall feel free at any time to respond to the request of the President of the College for advice on any matter pertaining to the College.

Section 4. In harmony with the provisions of this Article the (associate board) may have its own bylaws, subject to the approval of the Board of Trustees, and may elect its own officers.

ARTICLE VII—SEAL

The seal of the College shall be circular in shape, containing the name of the college, the year of founding and such device or shield as appear in the following impression.

---

[2] Sometimes called Board of Advisors, Board of Regents, President's Council, etc.

ARTICLE VIII—AMENDMENTS

These bylaws may be amended, repealed, or altered in whole or in part by a majority vote at any duly organized meeting of the Board of Trustees provided the proposed change is submitted in writing to each member at least ten (10) days before the time of meeting which is to consider the change.

The above bylaws were adopted at a meeting of the Board of Trustees on . . . .

Sample Administrative Charts

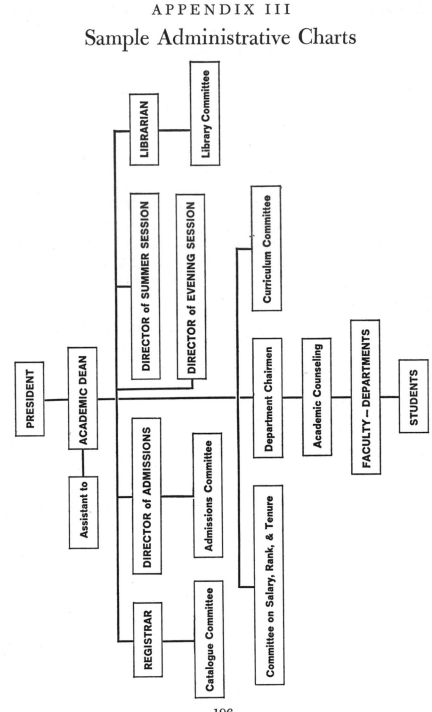

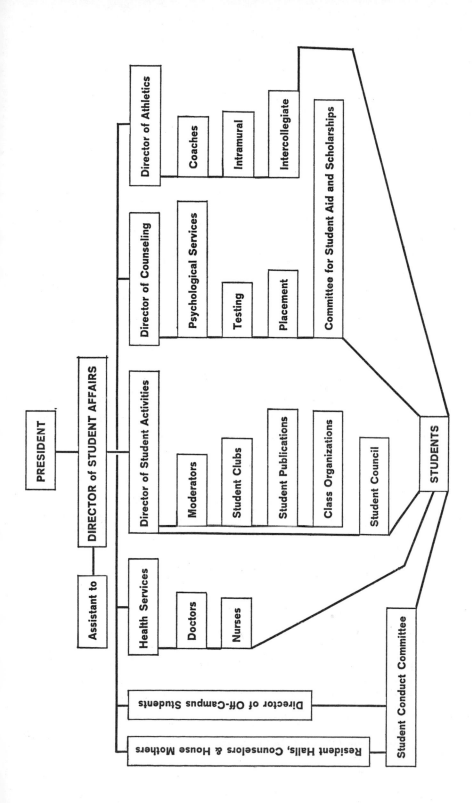

Bylaws of Administration*
Mythical College

ARTICLE I—NAME

The legal name of the corporation is MYTHICAL COLLEGE, hereinafter referred to as the College. The principal office of the College is in Fictitious, State of Jackson.

ARTICLE II—PURPOSE

The purpose of the College is to further the higher education of youths and adults and to confer such degrees upon the completion of such curricula as shall be established from time to time by the Board of Trustees and the faculty of the College, in accordance with the provisions of its charter and the laws of the State of Jackson.

ARTICLE III—BOARD OF TRUSTEES [1]

The Board of Trustees bears full and complete responsibility for the College as a corporate entity. It formulates and determines such general policies as may be deemed necessary for the administration and

---

* These BYLAWS do not include all officers found in even the smaller colleges but are presented for their suggestive value as to both form and content. Beyond this they will be useful only insofar as they can be adapted to the needs of a particular college.

[1] Sometimes called Board of Directors, Board of Overseers, etc.

development of the College. The property, affairs, business and concerns of the College are vested in the Board of Trustees, subject to the provisions of law and of the charter of the College.

ARTICLE IV—BOARD OF ASSOCIATES [2]

The Board of Associates is chosen by the Board of Trustees to assist in promoting the expansion and development of the College and to be concerned with such other matters as may be referred to it from time to time by the Board of Trustees.

ARTICLE V—THE PRESIDENT

The President is the chief executive of the College and is ultimately responsible for all its activities. While delegating duties and responsibilities to others, the President should undertake directly such responsibilities as the following:

1. Provide effective and stimulating educational leadership to staff, faculty and students.
2. See that all policies established by the Board of Trustees are implemented fully; that all legal requirements are met; that proper educational standards are observed; that everything possible is done to attain the stated objectives of the College, and to promote the best interests of students and faculty.
3. Report regularly to the Board of Trustees upon the condition of the College and make such recommendations as are considered expedient.
4. See that the annual budget is prepared for the approval of the Board of Trustees and also that it is administered properly.
5. Be personally concerned with the appointment of faculty members and determine their duties and salaries within whatever limits have been established by the Board of Trustees.
6. Appoint such officials,[3] department heads and committees as may prudently be deemed necessary for the efficient conduct of the College.
7. Be an *ex officio* member of all committees in the College.[4]

---

[2] Sometimes called President's Council, Board of Advisors, Board of Regents, etc.
[3] The President should have as much leeway as possible in the choice or selection of his principal assistants.
[4] A prudential measure, to be seldom used.

8. See that the faculty is kept informed as to trends in higher education and as to the development plans of the College.
9. Supervise all official publications of the College.
10. Promote good public relations with the community, the general public, sister colleges and secondary schools.
11. Represent the College to its constituencies, to the general public, to educational groups and agencies and, in general, be the spokesman in all external relations.
12. Develop and supervise plans for campus improvements, buildings and so on, as well as for the maintenance of grounds and buildings.
13. Supervise the raising of funds for the support and development of the College.

ARTICLE VI—THE ACADEMIC DEAN [5]

The Academic Dean is the chief academic officer of the College under the President and is directly responsible for all academic activities, with such specific responsibilities as the following:

1. Exercise general supervision over the faculty and be concerned with the efficient operation of the academic departments.
2. Supervise curricula, courses, methods of instructions, examinations and grading practices.
3. Recruit, when necessary, and interview and recommend to the President for appointment, competent faculty replacements and additions.
4. Assign teachers for service in a department and receive and approve their schedules for submission to the President.
5. In consultation with the Director of Admissions and the Committee on Admissions, recommend admission policies to the President.
6. See that policies concerning student achievement and deficiencies are carried out; approve students for degrees and, in general, supervise the academic welfare of students.
7. Preside at general faculty meetings whenever requested by the President and be an *ex officio* member of all faculty committees.
8. Prepare and keep up to date the Faculty Handbook and assist the President in supervising all official publications of the College.
9. Act as chief adviser to the President, and discharge the President's duties during his absence.

---

[5] Sometimes known as The Dean, Dean of the College, Dean of Studies, Vice President for Academic Affairs, etc. A qualification is advisable whenever other officers of the college also are called "Dean."

ARTICLE VII—DIRECTOR OF STUDENT AFFAIRS [6]

The Director of Student Affairs is the administrative officer directly responsible for the co-ordination and over-all development of the non-academic areas of student life. As the head of an important area of administration he has direct access to the President although he must collaborate and work closely with the Academic Dean. He has such duties as the following:

1. Serve as the liaison officer between the President and other administrative officers on all matters that concern the health, physical welfare, recreational and social needs of the students.
2. Exercise general supervision over non-academic counseling and placement services, inter-collegiate and intra-mural athletic, social and cultural activities.
3. Communicate with the faculty, student body, and general public on matters concerned with student life.
4. Recommend to the President persons who are deemed qualified to serve as house mothers, residence counselors, and faculty moderators for the various student activities.
5. Advise with faculty moderators of student activities about the definition, clarification, and development of policy for these activities.
6. Prepare the "Student Handbook," implement its rules and regulations as these pertain to student deportment, either on or off the campus.
7. Serve as an *ex officio* member of such faculty committees as are concerned with the non-academic interests of students and act as chairman of the committees on student conduct and student activities.
8. Work closely with the Student Council.
9. Make recommendations when necessary regarding maintenance and repair of such college facilities as are devoted to residential, dining and recreational needs of students.

---

[6] Sometimes called Director of Student Personnel Services, Dean of Students, Director of Student Relations, Vice President for Student Affairs, Dean of Men, Dean of Women, etc.

ARTICLE VIII—TREASURER-BUSINESS MANAGER [7]

The Treasurer-Business Manager who reports directly to the President, is charged with the supervision and control of the business activities and financial interests of the College and the management of its physical facilities. The Treasurer-Business Manager has such responsibilities as the following:

1. Supervise the collection of the income and revenues of the College, watch over its investments, and with proper authorization make payment from its funds to meet the various financial obligations of the College.
2. Maintain a proper system of bookkeeping and accounting and furnish such financial statements to the President and Board of Trustees as may be required.
3. Maintain and supervise an adequate system of central purchasing for all furnishings, equipment, supplies, etc.
4. Supervise the operation of the book store, snack-bar, dining room and any other income producing auxiliary enterprises.
5. Exercise direct control over all non-academic employees and supervise the maintenance of buildings and grounds.
6. Keep the President fully informed on the financial affairs of the College and on all important business and management problems as they may arise.
7. Prepare the annual budget in consultation with the President and, under his direction, exercise the necessary budget controls.

ARTICLE IX—DIRECTOR OF DEVELOPMENT AND PUBLIC RELATIONS [8]

The Director of Development, who reports directly to the President, heads up the area of administration which includes public relations, alumni relations, and all fund-raising activities of the College, whether for capital purposes, endowment, research, or current operations. More specifically the Director of Development is charged with such responsibilities as the following:

---

[7] Also called Bursar, Procurator, Vice President for Financial Affairs, Vice President for Business Management, etc.

[8] Sometimes known as Director of College Relations, Director of Public Relations and Development, Vice President for Development, Vice President for University Relations, Assistant to the President for Development, etc.

1. Plan and initiate, in close collaboration with the President, programs in public relations, voluntary support, and development, undertaking personally such of these activities as may be agreed upon.
2. Co-ordinate and supervise all activities of the College which have a bearing on public relations in its broadest sense, including news releases, student recruitment, alumni activities, etc.
3. Co-ordinate and supervise all activities which have any bearing on fund-raising and gifts and grants of any kind, including alumni fund-raising.
4. Maintain careful records of all gifts, grants, donations in cash or otherwise, made to any activity or department of the College, with full information as to their sources and purposes, and see that proper credit is given and due acknowledgment is made to the donors.

ARTICLE X—THE CHAPLAIN

The Chaplain is charged with the spiritual welfare of the students and has direct access to the President although most of his contacts will be with the Academic Dean and the Director of Student Affairs. He has such specific duties as the following:

1. Provide all regular and special religious services at the College.
2. Co-operate with the administration of the College in furthering the spiritual welfare of the students.
3. Act as spiritual adviser for those who seek this counsel.
4. Co-operate with such student religious activities as may be established.
5. Make such recommendations to the President as are calculated to promote the spiritual welfare of the students.

ARTICLE XI—THE LIBRARIAN

The Librarian is the custodian of all property of the Library, its books, papers, records and files. In conjunction with the Library Committee he shall formulate and administer such policies, rules and regulations as are calculated to secure the fullest use of the Library by students and faculty. The Librarian reports directly to the Academic Dean and has such responsibilities as the following:

1. Administer the Library in such a way as to render it a vital part of the institution's educational program.
2. Keep administration, faculty and students informed regularly of all new accessions to the Library and stimulate Library use in every way possible.
3. Keep records of circulation and Library use and make these available to administration and faculty.
4. Recommend annually the budget for salaries and for the purchase of books, periodicals, supplies and equipment.
5. Co-operate with appropriate inter-library projects and assist faculty members in obtaining photostats, microfilms, books, or other material on inter-library loan.
6. Be responsible for the long-range planning for the Library, its holdings, services and staff.

ARTICLE XII—THE REGISTRAR

The Registrar is concerned with the student from the time of actual acceptance as a student until the student leaves or is graduated from the College. Thereafter the Registrar is concerned with graduates or former students whenever there are requests for references or official transcripts of college records. The Registrar reports to the Academic Dean and has such duties as the following:

1. Take charge of all arrangements for the registration of students.
2. Schedule all classes and assign classrooms; plan teacher schedules in cooperation with the Academic Dean; section classes where required and set up student class schedules.
3. Make up such class lists, grade sheets and other student lists as may be required.
4. Receive and record all student grades, and compile class averages and ranks.
5. Prepare examination schedules as required.
6. Issue grade reports regularly to parents of students and to staff members when requested.
7. Keep all academic records and issue all transcripts in accordance with the College regulations.
8. Verify for the approval of the Academic Dean all candidates for academic honors and for graduation.
9. Prepare such statistical reports as may be considered useful or as may be requested by the President or Academic Dean.

10. Prepare the academic calendar of the College; collect the material and prepare the College catalogue for publication, in co-operation with the Academic Dean.

ARTICLE XIII—THE DIRECTOR OF ADMISSIONS

The Director of Admissions has the responsibility of recruiting students for the College and of receiving and processing applications in accordance with the established policies of the College. The Director of Admissions reports directly to the Academic Dean but maintains close relations with the Registrar and the Director of Development. The principal duties are:

1. Maintain contacts with high schools; arrange for faculty members to address high school student groups; arrange for participation in "college nights" where this is deemed appropriate; attend such college nights in person or arrange for satisfactory representation.
2. Supply information about the College to all inquirers, and supervise all correspondence relative to the admission of students.
3. Interview prospective students and their parents and arrange for campus tours.
4. With the advice of the Admissions Committee accept or decline applications and notify the applicants accordingly.
5. Make such statistical studies of applicants, acceptances and matriculants as may be considered useful or as may be requested by the President or Academic Dean.
6. Co-operate with the registrar so as to effect a smooth transition from applicant to registrant, to matriculant.

ARTICLE XIV—THE CHAIRMEN OF DEPARTMENTS

A department is a grouping of faculty members in one or more disciplines or subject-matter areas for both administrative and curricular purposes. No department is autonomous but each is a part of the whole college, linked together by a core curriculum and common administrators. Chairmen are appointed annually by the President in consultation with the Academic Dean and may be reappointed. Chairmen are immediately responsible to the Academic Dean for such duties as the following:

1. Prepare agenda for and preside at all departmental meetings once

each month during the academic year, or special meetings if such are required.

2. Forward the minutes of all departmental meetings to the President, the Academic Dean, the departmental faculty; and to all faculty members, if this is required.

3. Observe the work of the departmental faculty, especially of new members, and assist them in promoting the objectives of the College.

4. Encourage continued study for the doctorate or its departmental equivalent in the event that any faculty member does not have such a degree.

5. Draw up the teaching schedule of the departmental faculty subject to the approval of the Academic Dean.

6. Make recommendations to the Academic Dean regarding salary, promotion in rank and renewal of contracts of departmental faculty members.

7. Encourage active participation (and membership) in learned societies and professional organizations, and research and publication where possible.

8. Prepare, in consultation with the departmental faculty, recommendations for the revision of departmental objectives, programs, and course descriptions for the catalogue, in harmony with the general aims of the College.

9. Initiate revision of departmental curricula and submit such revision to the curriculum committee.

10. Supervise with the aid of the departmental faculty, the program of students majoring in the department.

11. Prepare, where required, and submit in writing to the Academic Dean a departmental budget for the coming year.

12. Confer with the Academic Dean relative to the need for new staff members, review applications for vacancies, and interview applicants.

13. Co-operate with the Librarian in the improvement of library holdings relative to the department and promote the use of the library by faculty and students in the department.

14. Be responsible, in co-operation with the college bookstore, for the procurement of all text books prescribed for departmental courses.

15. Maintain all appropriate records of the department, including syllabi of all departmental courses.

16. Co-operate in every way with the Academic Dean in carrying out the program and furthering the objectives of the College.

ARTICLE XV—THE ADMINISTRATIVE COUNCIL

The Administrative Council is a top-level committee comprised of the President as chairman, the Academic Dean, the Director of Student Affairs, the Treasurer-Business Manager, and the Director of Development. Its primary function is to maintain good communication among the chief administrators, to smooth out any points of friction, and to promote close co-operation. It serves also in an advisory capacity to the President. In line with these functions the Council has such activities as the following:

1. To hold regular weekly meetings at which there shall be brief oral reports by each administrator.
2. To serve, when requested as a clearing house for proposals from other committees and departments.
3. To recommend policies and procedures that affect the College as a whole.
4. To consider such other matters pertaining to the College as may be proposed by the President.

ARTICLE XVI—COMMITTEES

There shall be the following four standing committees comprised of *ex officio* and appointed (or elected) members: Admissions; Curriculum; Student Conduct; Scholarships and Student Aid. Appointments are for one year terms with privilege of reappointment. (Elections are for two years.)

In addition to the standing committees the President shall appoint, or authorize the appointment of *ad hoc* committees whenever this seems desirable.

ARTICLE XVII—COMMITTEE ON ADMISSIONS

The Committee on Admissions shall consist of the Director of Admissions as chairman, the Academic Dean, and two or more faculty representatives of the departments to be appointed by the President. The formal acceptance or non-acceptance of all applicants to the College shall be made in the name of the Committee on Admissions. But this does not mean that the committee must act formally and individually on each applicant. Thus the committee should:

1. Delegate to the Director of Admissions certain discretionary powers to accept without formal committee action applicants who definitely meet the stated requirements and to decline applicants who clearly fail to meet requirements.
2. Agree on a procedure whereby the Admissions office can refer to the Committee applicants whose qualifications are doubtful, or whose credentials require review or special examination.
3. Recommend to the Academic Dean and President changes or modifications in admission standards and procedures.

ARTICLE XVIII—COMMITTEE ON CURRICULUM

The Committee on Curriculum shall consist of the Academic Dean as chairman, the Registrar and four members of the faculty to be appointed by the President, representing the humanities, the natural sciences, the social sciences and philosophy and religion. It shall be the duty of the committee to:

1. Advise and assist the Academic Dean in building and maintaining a curriculum constructed to attain best the objectives of the College.
2. Consider departmental recommendations for curriculum changes presented to it in writing.
3. Submit for the approval of the Administrative Council recommendations for changes and improvements in curriculum, testing and grading practices, teaching methods and other instructional matters having a bearing on the effectiveness of the curriculum.

ARTICLE XIX—COMMITTEE ON STUDENT CONDUCT

The Committee on Student Conduct shall consist of the Director of Student Affairs as chairman, the Academic Dean, the Residence Hall Counselors, the Moderator of non-resident students, and two other Faculty members who are not directly connected with student activities. The Committee shall be responsible for student conduct in general. Specifically it shall be the function of the committee to:

1. Formulate for the approval of the President rules and regulations to govern student discipline on and off the campus.
2. Set up a procedure for dealing with the less grave student infractions of discipline.
3. Grant hearings to students accused of the more grave disciplinary

infractions, pass judgment and, where indicated, invoke such sanctions as suspension or expulsion, with the understanding that these become effective only with the approval of the President.

4. Inform in writing, through the chairman of the committee, the parents of any student who has become a disciplinary problem or who gives promise of becoming one.

ARTICLE XX—COMMITTEE ON SCHOLARSHIPS AND STUDENT AID

The Committee on Scholarships and Student Aid shall consist of the Registrar as chairman, the Academic Dean, the Director of Admissions, the Treasurer-Business Manager and one member of the faculty to be appointed by the President. It shall be the duty of this committee to:

1. Organize the scholarship and student aid program.
2. Examine applications for financial assistance and grant or deny, renew or withdraw, any scholarship, grant-in-aid, or other assistance, according as the circumstances in individual cases may warrant.

ARTICLE XXI—THE FACULTY

1. In addition to administrators, the faculty shall consist of professors, associate professors, assistant professors, and instructors, who have been duly appointed on a full-time basis. Part-time members of the faculty shall be either lecturers or part-time instructors.
2. Members of the faculty shall have the rights, privileges, duties and responsibilities that are customarily found in other similar colleges. They shall have freedom of research and publication and of classroom discussion, but they shall not be free to disseminate doctrines and views that are subversive of the basic principles of American freedom and government or of the aims and purposes of the College as a Catholic institution committed to uphold the principles of Christian faith and morality.

ARTICLE XXII—FACULTY DUTIES AND RESPONSIBILITIES

Faculty members shall co-operate to the best of their abilities with the officials of the College in promoting the welfare of students and in seeking to attain the objectives of the institution. Particularly are they expected to:

1. Report at College before the opening of the academic year on the date designated by the President or the Academic Dean.
2. Attend the assigned classes faithfully throughout the college year and make themselves regularly available for student consultations.
3. Assist in departmental and committee work and act as moderators of student activities when requested.
4. Attend departmental and general faculty meetings and such public college functions as may be required.
5. Uphold the professed ideals of the College and co-operate with the President and other officials of the College in promoting its objectives.
6. If full-time members of the faculty, not engage in any outside employment or occupation without the knowledge and consent of the President, and then only when it does not interfere with the thorough, efficient, and earnest performance of college duties.

ARTICLE XXIII—THE SEAL OF THE COLLEGE

The seal of the College shall be circular in shape, containing the name of the College and such device or shield as appear in the following impression:

ARTICLE XXIV—AMENDMENTS

These Bylaws may be amended, repealed, or altered in whole or in part by a majority vote of the Board of Trustees at any regular or special meeting, provided that notice of the proposed change is sent to the Trustees not later than the notice of the meeting which is to consider the change.

The above Bylaws were adopted at a meeting of the Board of Trustees on. . . . .

ADDENDUM

If a college provides limited graduate work in making it possible for teachers, for example, to qualify for a Master's degree in Education, this should be reflected in the BYLAWS. In this event the two following ARTICLES can be added to the BYLAWS. An ARTICLE XIV—DIRECTOR OF GRADUATE STUDY, can follow immediately after DIRECTOR OF ADMISSIONS, with the renumbering of the Articles following. An ARTICLE XVII—THE GRADUATE COUNCIL, could follow immediately after THE ADMINISTRATIVE COUNCIL, with the renumbering of the Articles following.

ARTICLE XIV—DIRECTOR OF GRADUATE STUDY

The Director of Graduate Study shall have charge of all matters pertaining to graduate studies and shall be directly responsible to the Academic Dean. It is the responsibility of the Director to:

1. Admit or refuse candidates for graduate work in collaboration with the Director of Admissions.
2. See that Graduate Record, Language, and Comprehensive examinations are properly administered.
3. Give final approval of subjects for dissertations.
4. Accept dissertations upon the recommendation of the candidate's adviser.
5. Make recommendations to the Academic Dean with respect to staff and equipment and submit a budget when required.
6. Preside at meetings of the Graduate Council.
7. Co-operate with the Registrar in the production of the catalogue for Graduate Studies.
8. Work with the President and the Academic Dean to promote harmony and cooperation between graduate and undergraduate operations.

ARTICLE XVII—THE GRADUATE COUNCIL

The Graduate Council shall be composed of the Director of Graduate Study as chairman, the Academic Dean, and the professors in charge of graduate majors. The Council has the general task of promoting high standards of graduate study without prejudice in any way to the pursuit of excellence in the undergraduate courses. Its decisions shall be subject to approval of the Administrative Council. The chief responsibilities of the Graduate Council are to:

1. Organize and review continuously the program of graduate studies.
2. Consider and weigh all requests for the extension of graduate work and recommend to the Administrative Council the acceptance, denial, or postponement of such requests.
3. Approve candidates for degrees upon the recommendation of the Director.
4. Recommend to the Administrative Council all rules and regulations affecting graduate studies.
5. Consider such other matters affecting the graduate studies as may be proposed by the Director.

NOTE. The Bylaws of Administration presented on the preceeding pages *do not include* all the administrative officers which normally would have to be included in the bylaws of a specific college. Thus, a number of officers included in the administrative charts on pages 196 and 197 have been omitted. This has been done so as not to lengthen unduly this "sample" set of bylaws. It is felt that enough has been included to illustrate the purpose and use of bylaws of administration.

APPENDIX V

Sample Policies
for Faculty Appointments, etc.

A COLLEGE ought to have definite statements of policy on *Faculty Appointments, Termination of Appointments, Tenure, Rank and Promotion.* These should be available in printed form either as a separate document, or included in the FACULTY HANDBOOK. The following sample policy statements are presented for their suggestive value.

A. FACULTY APPOINTMENTS

1. Every appointment of a faculty member shall be made by a formal agreement signed by him and by the president of the college or his representative, and shall state the rank, salary, length of agreement, and other conditions of appointment. A copy of the terms of appointment shall be presented to each prospective faculty member prior to his acceptance of appointment. Acceptance of the appointment shall be considered to indicate the appointee's willingness to be bound by all the terms of the agreement.

2. Appointments shall be of two kinds: temporary or *term* appointments and permanent or *continuous* appointments. Term appointments terminate at the close of the period specifically stated in the agreement. These appointments are subject to renewal but carry no obligation either on the college or on the appointee, for reappointment. Con-

213

tinuous appointments carry assurance of permanency until retirement age has been reached and are subject to termination only under conditions mutually understood and accepted at the time of appointment.

3. New members of the faculty shall be engaged initially on a term appointment. Renewal of term appointments shall be for one year or not more than two years until a continuous appointment is made. Usually faculty members who hold the rank of professor or associate professor are considered to have continuous appointments. Interim semester appointments and appointments as lecturer or part-time instructor, are always term appointments.

4. All renewals of term appointments shall be given by March 1 of the final year specified in the agreement, and shall be signed by the faculty member and returned to the president by April 1. In the case of continuous appointments, no renewal is required. Nevertheless faculty contract forms will be issued to all faculty members because they specify salary payments, deductions and the like which are subject to change. These should also be signed and returned.

5. Notice of intention not to reappoint will be given by February 1st of the final year specified in the agreement. A faculty member who proposes to withdraw shall give notice at least by April 1 of the contract year.

B. TERMINATION OF FACULTY APPOINTMENTS

1. Faculty appointments terminate normally by the expiration of the specified length of the appointment in the case of *term* appointments and by "retirement for age" in the case of *continuous* appointments.

2. Appointments, both *term* and *continuous,* may be terminated before their expiration:

(a) By the president or board of trustees for such causes as: conviction in the courts for a serious crime, grave moral delinquency, professional incompetence, physical or mental incapacity, and flagrant defiance of the ideals of the college.

(b) By the faculty member, by resignation given in writing by April 1, and to take effect at the end of the current school year.

(c) By mutual agreement in cases not covered in (a) and (b).

3. Dismissal for reasons other than moral delinquency shall take effect at the end of the semester next following the semester in which the initial written notice of intention to sever relations is given. Dismissal for moral delinquency shall take effect immediately.

4. Termination of appointment for the causes given in (a) above shall be considered by the Administrative Council and by a specially appointed faculty appeal board before final action is taken by the president or the board of trustees. The final decision in all cases shall rest with the board of trustees.

5. The continuous appointment of a faculty member shall terminate at the close of the school term during which he reaches his sixty-fifth birthday. Thereafter his service to the college may be extended at the option of the board of trustees, on an annual or semi-annual basis, for full or part-time work, as may suit the convenience of the college and on such terms as may be mutually agreed upon.

C. FACULTY TENURE

1. Tenure means the assurance of continuous appointment until retirement age has been reached and is subject only to termination for cause under conditions mutually understood and accepted at the time of appointment.

2. Tenure shall be granted to a faculty member upon promotion to the rank of professor provided he has served at least three years at the College. It may be granted also to one who holds the rank of associate professor provided he has served at least four years at the College. An assistant professor who has served at least seven years at the College may be granted tenure upon the special recommendation of the Administrative Council. In case of initial appointment of a faculty member to the rank of professor or associate professor, tenure shall ordinarily not begin until after three years of service at the College. In exceptional cases it may be granted immediately to an experienced faculty member who transfers to the college from another college.

3. Loss of tenure can be occasioned (a) by such causes as: conviction in the courts for a serious crime, grave moral delinquency, professional incompetence, mental or physical incapacity, and flagrant defiance of the ideals of the college, on the part of the faculty member, and (b) by financial stringency on the part of the college which is demonstrably in good faith.

D. FACULTY RANK AND PROMOTION

1. Teaching members of the faculty appointed on a full-time basis, may be assigned to one of four ranks on the strength of their graduate training, their years of experience, and testimony as to their profes-

sional competence. These ranks in ascending order are: instructor, assistant professor, associate professor and professor.

2. There is no limit on the number of years which a faculty member may serve in a given rank. Promotion from one rank to another is not automatic, and only under exceptional circumstances will it be made at less than three year intervals. Promotion from one rank to another requires recommendations based on the evaluation of certain criteria. Advancement to the rank of associate professor or professor requires in addition that an appropriate opening be available.

3. The following *criteria* are to be considered in making recommendations: (1) graduate training; (2) years of service; (3) fidelity and ability as a teacher; (4) effectiveness in counseling; (5) efforts in departmental and committee work within the college; (6) ability to uphold the ideals of the college, to promote its objectives, and to co-operate with others to that end; (7) scholarly interests, publications and research.

4. Expressed in terms of both quantitative and qualitative criteria, the basis for appointment or advancement may be stated for each rank as follows:

An *instructor* shall have the M.A. degree or its equivalent, or substantial progress toward a graduate degree, and also possess character and personality traits that will contribute to effective teaching. Previous college teaching shall be preferred but not required. An *assistant professor* shall have the M.A. degree and substantial progress toward the doctorate or its equivalent, at least three years of successful college teaching or its equivalent, and an acceptable rating on the qualitative criteria items (3) to (7) inclusive, given above.

An *associate professor* shall have the Ph.D. degree or its equivalent, at least six years of successful college teaching or its equivalent, and an acceptable rating on the qualitative criteria items (3) to (7) inclusive.

A *professor* shall have the Ph.D. degree or its equivalent, at least nine years of successful college teaching or its equivalent, and an acceptable rating on the qualitative criteria items (3) to (7) inclusive.

5. Recommendations for promotion may be initiated by the department chairman before January 1. Each recommendation shall include a written evaluation of the faculty member's work together with rea-

sons favoring promotion, and shall be presented to the dean. The dean may add his comments and present all the information to the Administrative Council which shall make its own recommendations to the president of the college. Final approval will rest with the president if he has been delegated this authority by the board of trustees; otherwise it will depend on the board itself.

6. A faculty member appointed on a part-time basis shall be designated: (a) *lecturer*, if he holds the Ph.D degree or its equivalent in his field and holds, or has held, professional rank in another institution of college level, or is an outstanding leader in his professional field; (b) part-time instructor, if he does not qualify as a lecturer, but holds an M.A. degree or its equivalent in his field or has achieved some distinction in his professional field.

APPENDIX VI

Sample Statements of Fund Transactions

THE BALANCE sheet, as explained on pages 155-157, is a statement of the conditions of each fund group, showing assets, liabilities, and fund balances as of the date of the report. The fund balances result from various transactions during the year, and these should be reported in supporting schedules. The schedules should show, separately by each fund group, the balance at the beginning of the fiscal year; additions during the year because of receipts, transfers, income, or other forms of credits; deductions during the year for disbursements, transfers, expenditures and other forms of charges; and the balance at the end of the year.

Our discussion will be confined to the fund groups which appear on the Condensed Balance Sheet on page 156; namely, current funds, loan funds, endowment funds and plant funds. Most institutions will have at least these funds. Sample supporting statements for each fund will also be presented.

I. CURRENT FUNDS

The statement for the current funds group is frequently referred to as the Statement of Current Funds Balance. Beginning with the balance from the past year this statement will show under "Additions During Year" such items as—(a) the excess of current income over current expenditures described on page 161.

(b) *Transfers*. These do not occur frequently but occasionally there are transactions which add to Current Funds Balance but which are not current income. An example would be the release of an undesignated and unrestricted Annuity Fund upon the termination of the annuity agreement through the death of the annuitant. Such an Annuity Fund might be transferred to Current Funds Balance upon appropriate action of the board of trustees, and would be recorded as an addition to that account.

"Deductions During Year" include such items as —(a) The excess of current expenditures over current income, if that condition prevails, the figures coming from the statements of current income and current expenditures described on pages 158, 160.

(b) *Transfers*. Current Funds frequently are transferred to other fund groups. The practice is becoming more and more general for colleges to use current funds,—the excess of current income over current expenditures,—to help meet growing needs for plant expansion. Also, the net income, either in whole or in part, from the operations of dormitories, dining halls, and other auxiliary enterprises, frequently is used to meet amortization costs of the buildings. Such transfers should be shown as additions to Plant Funds, and charged against Current Funds Balance rather than as items in the statement of current expenditures. Under the regulations governing the NDEA loan funds, colleges must appropriate some of their own funds to supplement the governmental grant. If current funds are used for this purpose, the

SUMMARY STATEMENT OF CURRENT FUNDS BALANCE

Balance Beginning of Year		$25,518.78
Additions During Year—		
Excess of Current Income Over Current Expenditures—		
Current Income	$581,178.82	
Current Expenditures	578,297.68	
		2,881.14
Transfers (Smith Annuity)		9,912.00
Sub-Total		$38,311.92
Deductions During Year—		
Excess of Current Expenditures Over Current Income—		
Transfers—		
To Plant Funds	$ 18,000.00	
To Loan Funds	911.00	18,911.00
Balance End of Year		$19,400.92

transfer to the Loan Funds group should appear as a charge against Current Funds Balance.

On p. 219 is an illustration of the form of the Statement of Current Funds Balance.

II. LOAN FUNDS

"Additions During Year" include: (a) Gift and bequests of funds designated for loaning purposes; (b) Income from endowment funds designated for loaning purposes; (c) Interest on loan notes; (d) Governmental grants, such as NDEA funds; and (e) Transfers from other funds or fund groups; for example, the institutional appropriation required by the NDEA program.

"Deductions During Year" include: (a) Notes written off; (b) Legal expense involved in the collection of notes; and (c) Any other charges against the principal or balances of Loan Funds. The granting of loans and the repayment of notes do *not* constitute receipts or disbursements of Loan Funds. An illustration of the form of the Statement of Loan Funds follows:

SUMMARY STATEMENT OF LOAN FUNDS

Balance Beginning of Year		$32,529.00
Additions During Year—		
Gifts and Bequests	$ — —	
Interest on Loans	— —	
Governmental Grants	$8,200.00	
Transfer From Current Funds	911.00	9,111.00
Sub-Total		$41,640.00
Deductions During Year—		
Notes Written Off	600.00	
Other	— —	600.00
Balance End of Year		$41,040.00

III. ENDOWMENT FUNDS

"Additions During Year" include: (a) Gifts and bequests designated for endowment purposes, the income only to be expended or used; (b) Investment income added to the principal of endowment Funds in accordance with the terms of gifts and bequests; (c) Net gains during the year on investment transactions; and (d) Transfers from other fund groups.

"Deductions During Year" include: (a) Net losses during the year on investment transactions; (b) Transfers to other fund groups; and (c) Other charges against the principal of endowment funds.

The purchase and sale of investments of endowment funds do *not* constitute receipts and disbursements of the funds. An illustration of the form of the Statement of Endowment Funds follows:

SUMMARY STATEMENT OF ENDOWMENT FUNDS

Balance Beginning of Year		$316,100.00
Additions During Year—		
Gifts and Bequests	$10,000.00	
Income Added To Principal	1,100.00	
Net Gains on Investment Transactions	— —	
Transfers From Other Funds		11,100.00
Sub-Total		$327,200.50
Deductions During Year—		
Net Losses on Investment Transactions	500.00	
Transfers and Other Charges		500.00
Balance End of Year		$326,700.50

IV. Plant Funds

Three statements of fund transactions are necessary for the Plant Funds group; one for the funds designated for use in plant expansion but not yet expended; another for funds set aside for the retirement of indebtedness on the plant; and a third for the funds expended for plant facilities.

A. *Unexpended Plant Funds.* "Additions During Year" include such items as: (a) Gifts, bequests, and grants specifically earmarked for plant purposes; (b) Government appropriation for plant purposes; (c) Earnings and profits on the temporary investment of Plant Funds; (d) Transfer from other fund groups; and (e) Proceeds from borrowings for plant purposes.

"Deductions During Year" would include such items as: (a) Amounts expended for plant facilities; that is, payments to contractors on construction contracts; or payments for the purchase of land, buildings, or other plant assets. These deductions should be grouped by type of assets, such as, land, buildings, improvements other than buildings, equipment, etc.

The form of the Statement of Unexpended Plant Funds is as follows:

SUMMARY STATEMENT OF UNEXPENDED PLANT FUNDS

Balance Beginning of Year		$ 23,260.98
Additions During Year—		
Gifts, Bequests and Grants	$ 40,000.00	
Transfers From Other Funds	— —	
Proceeds from Borrowings for Plant Purposes	200,000.00	240,000.00
Sub-Total		$263,260.98
Deductions During Year—		
Expended For Buildings	$200,000.00	
Equipment	40,000.00	
Land	23,000.00	263,000.00
Balance End of Year		$ 260.98

B. *Funds for Debt Retirement.* "Additions During Year" include: (a) Transfers from other groups. For example, the amount transferred from Current Fund Surplus to be used for debt retirement; the net income from operations of auxiliary enterprises to be used for debt service and financial expenses, should be reported here as additions to the Funds for Debt Retirement. (b) Income from the temporary investment of these funds; and (c) Other additions to funds which are to be used for the retirement of indebtedness on the plant facilities.

"Deductions During Year" include such items as: (a) Principal payments on indebtedness; and (b) Trustee charges and other similar financial expenses related to the indebtedness on the plant.

The Statement of Funds for Debt Retirement would appear as follows:

SUMMARY STATEMENT OF FUNDS FOR DEBT RETIREMENT

Balance Beginning of Year		$285,000.00
Additions During Year—		
Transfers From Current Funds Surplus	$ 18,000.00	
Transfers From Other Fund Groups	— —	18,000.00
Sub-Total		$303,000.00
Deductions During Year—		
Principal Payments	$300,000.00	300,000.00
Balance End of Year		$ 3,000.00

C. *Net Investment on Plant.* "Additions During Year" include: (a) Amounts expended from Plant Funds. (Shown as Deductions During Year in the Summary Statement of Unexpended Plant Funds); (b) Amounts expended from Current Funds and included in the Statement of Current Expenditures. These are items of equipment, furniture and fixtures, and apparatus for which Current Funds have been budgeted and expended; they usually are of relatively small amounts and occur generally in the current operations of the college each year. Reporting these items as additions to the Net Investment in Plant account reflects the "capitalization" in the Plant Funds Section of the value of permanent equipment acquired through the expenditure of Current Funds. (c) Appraised value of gifts of plant assets. (d) Amount of debt retired as shown in the Summary Statement of Funds for Debt Retirement.

"Deductions During Year" include: (a) Plant assets sold, written off, or otherwise disposed of. The Statement for Net Investment in Plant would appear as follows:

SUMMARY STATEMENT OF NET INVESTMENT IN PLANT

Balance Beginning of Year		$1,185.121.60
Additions During Year—		
Expended From Plant Funds	$263,000.00	
Expended From Current Funds	3,000.00	
Gifts Of Plant Assets	45,000.00	
Debt Retired	300,000.00	611,000.00
Sub-Total		$1,796,121.00
Deductions During Year—		
Plant Assets Disposed of		2,000.00
Balance End of Year		$1,794,121.60

APPENDIX VII

Association of American Colleges, Statements on Academic Freedom and Tenure, and Dismissal Proceedings

Reprinted from ASSOCIATION OF AMERICAN COLLEGES BULLETIN, Volume XXVII, Number 1, March, 1941, pages 124-125 and 127-129.

ACADEMIC FREEDOM AND TENURE

[Statement of principles formulated by joint conferences of the Commission on Academic Freedom and Academic Tenure with the officers of the American Association of University Professors and endorsed by the Association of American Colleges at the annual meeting held in Pasadena, January 10, 1941.]

The purpose of this statement is to promote public understanding and support of academic freedom and tenure and agreement upon procedures to assure them in colleges and universities. Institutions of higher education are conducted for the common good and not to further the interest of either the individual teacher* or the institution as a whole. The common good depends upon the free search for truth and its free exposition.

Academic freedom is essential to these purposes and applies to both teaching and research. Freedom in research is fundamental to the advancement of truth. Academic freedom in its teaching aspect is

---

* The word "teacher" as used in this document is understood to include the investigator who is attached to an academic institution without teaching duties.

fundamental for the protection of the rights of the teacher in teaching and of the student to freedom in learning. It carries with it duties correlative with rights.

Tenure is a means to certain ends; specifically: (1) Freedom of teaching and research and of extra-mural activities, and (2) a sufficient degree of economic security to make the profession attractive to men and women of ability. Freedom and economic security, hence tenure, are indispensable to the success of an institution in fulfilling its obligations to its students and to society.

Academic Freedom

(a) The teacher is entitled to full freedom in research and in the publication of the results, subject to the adequate performance of his other academic duties; but research for pecuniary return should be based upon an understanding with the authorities of the institution.

(b) The teacher is entitled to freedom in the classroom in discussing his subject, but he should be careful not to introduce into his teaching controversial matter which has no relation to his subject. Limitations of academic freedom because of religious or other aims of the institution should be clearly stated in writing at the time of the appointment.

(c) The college or university teacher is a citizen, a member of a learned profession, and an officer of an educational institution. When he speaks or writes as a citizen, he should be free from institutional censorship or discipline, but his special position in the community imposes special obligations. As a man of learning and an educational officer, he should remember that the public may judge his profession and his institution by his utterances. Hence he should at all times be accurate, should exercise appropriate restraint, should show respect for the opinions of others, and should make every effort to indicate that he is not an institutional spokesman.

Academic Tenure

(a) After the expiration of a probationary period teachers or investigators should have permanent or continuous tenure, and their services should be terminated only for adequate cause, except in the case of retirement for age, or under extraordinary circumstances because of financial exigencies.

(b) In the interpretation of this principle it is understood that the following represents acceptable academic practice:

(1) The precise terms and conditions of every appointment should be stated in writing and be in the possession of both institution and teacher before the appointment is consummated.

(2) Beginning with appointment to the rank of full-time instructor or a higher rank, the probationary period should not exceed seven years, including within this period full-time service in all institutions of higher education; but subject to the proviso that when, after a term of probationary service of more than three years in one or more institutions, a teacher is called to another institution it may be agreed in writing that his new appointment is for a probationary period of not more than four years, even though thereby the person's total probationary period in the academic profession is extended beyond the normal maximum of seven years. Notice should be given at least one year prior to the expiration of the probationary period, if the teacher is not to be continued in service after the expiration of that period.

(3) During the probationary period a teacher should have the academic freedom that all other members of the faculty have.

(4) Termination for cause of a continuous appointment, or the dismissal for cause of a teacher previous to the expiration of a term appointment, should, if possible, be considered by both a faculty committee and the governing board of the institution. In all cases where the facts are in dispute, the accused teacher should be informed before the hearing in writing of the charges against him and should have the opportunity to be heard in his own defense by all bodies that pass judgment upon his case. He should be permitted to have with him an adviser of his own choosing who may act as counsel. There should be a full stenographic record of the hearing available to the parties concerned. In the hearing of charges of incompetence the testimony should include that of teachers and other scholars, either from his own or from other institutions. Teachers on continuous appointment who are dismissed for reasons not involving moral turpitude should receive their salaries for at least a year from the date of notification of dismissal whether or not they are continued in their duties at the institution.

(5) Termination of a continuous appointment because of financial exigency should be demonstrably bona fide.

INTERPRETATIONS

The following interpretations concerning the joint statement on academic freedom and tenure were agreed upon:

I

First: That its operation should not be retroactive.

II

Second: That all tenure claims of teachers appointed prior to its endorsement should be determined in accordance with the principles set forth in the 1925 statement on academic freedom and tenure.

III

Third: If the administration of a college or university feels that a teacher has not observed the admonitions of Paragraph (c) of the section on *Academic Freedom* and believes that the extramural utterances of the teacher have been such as to raise grave doubts concerning his fitness for his position, it may proceed to file charges under Paragraph (b) (4) of the section on *Academic Tenure*. In pressing such charges the administration should remember that teachers are citizens and should be accorded the freedom of citizens. In such cases the administration must assume full responsibility and the American Association of University Professors and the Association of American Colleges are free to make an investigation.

STATEMENT ON PROCEDURAL STANDARDS IN FACULTY DISMISSAL PROCEEDINGS

Reprinted from ASSOCIATION OF AMERICAN COLLEGES BULLETIN, Volume XLIV, Number 1, March, 1958, pages 122-130.

Introductory Comments

This statement deals with procedural standards. Those recommended are not intended to establish a norm in the same manner as the 1940 Statement of Principles of Academic Freedom and Tenure, but are presented rather as a guide to be used according to the nature and traditions of particular institutions in giving effect to both faculty tenure rights and the obligations of faculty members in the academic community.

Procedural Recommendations

1. Preliminary Proceedings Concerning the Fitness of a Faculty Member

When reason arises to question the fitness of a college or university faculty member who has tenure or whose term appointment has not expired, the appropriate administrative officers should ordinarily discuss the matter with him in personal conference. The matter may be terminated by mutual consent at this point; but if an adjustment does not result, a standing or ad hoc committee elected by the faculty and charged with the function of rendering confidential advice in such situations, should informally inquire into the situation, to effect an adjustment if possible and, if none is effected, to determine whether in its view formal proceedings to consider his dismissal should be instituted. If the committee recommends that such proceedings should be begun, or if the president of the institution, even after considering a recommendation of the committee favorable to the faculty member, expresses his conviction that a proceeding should be undertaken, action should be commenced under the procedures which follow. Except where there is disagreement, a statement with reasonable particularity of the grounds proposed for the dismissal should then be jointly formulated by the president and the faculty committee; if there is disagreement, the president or his representative should formulate the statement.

2. Commencement of Formal Proceedings

The formal proceedings should be commenced by a communication addressed to the faculty member by the president of the institution, informing the faculty member of the statement formulated, and informing him that if he so requests, a hearing to determine whether he should be removed from his faculty position on the grounds stated will be conducted by a faculty committee at a specified time and place. In setting the date of the hearing, sufficient time should be allowed the faculty member to prepare his defense. The faculty member should be informed, in detail or by reference to published regulations, of the procedural rights that will be accorded to him. The faculty member should state in reply whether he wishes a hearing and, if so, should answer in writing, not less than one week before the date set for the hearing, the statements in the president's letter.

3. Suspension of the Faculty Member

Suspension of the faculty member during the proceedings involving him is justified only if immediate harm to himself or others is threatened by his continuance. Unless legal considerations forbid, any such suspension should be with pay.

4. Hearing Committee

The committee of faculty members to conduct the hearing and reach a decision should either be an elected standing committee not previously concerned with the case or a committee established as soon as possible after the president's letter to the faculty member has been sent. The choice of members of the hearing committee should be on the basis of their objectivity and competence and of the regard in which they are held in the academic community. The committee should elect its own chairman.

5. Committee Proceeding

The committee should proceed by considering the statement of grounds for dismissal already formulated, and the faculty member's response written before the time of the hearing. If the faculty member has not requested a hearing, the committee should consider the case on the basis of the obtainable information and decide whether he should be removed; otherwise the hearing should go forward. The committee, in consultation with the president and the faculty member, should exercise its judgment as to whether the hearing should be public or private. If any facts are in dispute, the testimony of witnesses and other evidence concerning the matter set forth in the president's letter to the faculty member should be received.

The president should have the option of attendance during the hearing. He may designate an appropriate representative to assist in developing the case; but the committee should determine the order of proof, should normally conduct the questioning of witnesses, and, if necessary, should secure the presentation of evidence important to the case.

The faculty member should have the option of assistance by counsel, whose functions should be similar to those of the representative chosen by the president. The faculty member should have the additional procedural rights set forth in the 1940 Statement of Principles of Academic Freedom and Tenure, and should have the aid of the committee, when needed, in securing the attendance of witnesses. The faculty member or his counsel and the representative designated by the president should have the right within reasonable limits to question all witnesses who testify orally. The faculty member should have the opportunity to be confronted by all witnesses adverse to him. Where unusual and urgent reasons move the hearing committee to withhold this right, or where the witness cannot appear, the identity of the witness, as well as his statement, should nevertheless be disclosed to the faculty member. Subject to these safeguards, statements may when necessary be taken outside the hearing and reported to it. All of the evidence should be duly recorded. Unless special circumstances warrant, it should not be necessary to follow formal rules of court procedure.

6. Consideration by Hearing Committee

The committee should reach its decision in conference, on the basis of the hearing. Before doing so, it should give opportunity to the faculty member or his counsel and the representative designated by the president to argue orally before it. If written briefs would be helpful, the committee may request them. The committee may proceed to decision promptly, without having the record of the hearing transcribed, where it feels that a just decision can be reached by this means; or it may await the availability of a transcript of the hearing if its decision would be aided thereby. It should make explicit findings with respect to each of the grounds of removal presented, and a reasoned opinion may be desirable. Publicity concerning the committee's decision may properly be withheld until consideration has been given to the case by the governing body of the institution. The president and the faculty member should be notified of the decision in writing and should be given a copy of the record of the hearing. Any release to the public should be made through the president's office.

7. Consideration by Governing Body

The president should transmit to the governing body the full report of the hearing committee, stating its action. On the assumption that the governing board has accepted the principle of the faculty hearing committee, acceptance of the committee's decision would normally be expected. If the governing body chooses to review the case, its review should be based on the record of the previous hearing, accompanied by opportunity for argument, oral or written or both, by the principals at the hearing or their representatives. The decision of the hearing committee should either be sustained or the proceeding be returned to the committee with objections specified. In such a case the committee should reconsider, taking account of the stated objections and receiving new evidence if necessary. It should frame its decision and communicate it in the same manner as before. Only after study of the committee's reconsideration should the governing body make a final decision overruling the committee.

8. Publicity

Except for such simple announcements as may be required, covering the time of the hearing and similar matters, public statements about the case by either the faculty member or administrative officers should be avoided so far as possible until the proceedings have been completed. Announcement of the final decision should include a statement of the hearing committee's original action, if this has not previously been made known.

Index

233